The International Library of Sociology

LEGAL AID

Founded by KARL MANNHEIM

The International Library of Sociology

THE SOCIOLOGY OF LAW AND CRIMINOLOGY
In 15 Volumes

I	Comparative Criminology (Part One)	*Mannheim*
II	Comparative Criminology (Part Two)	*Mannheim*
III	Crime: An Analytical Appraisal	*Lopez-Rey*
IV	The Criminal Area	*Morris*
V	Criminal Justice and Social Reconstruction	*Mannheim*
VI	The Education of Borstal Boys	*Stratta*
VII	The English Prison and Borstal Systems	*Fox*
VIII	The Explanation of Criminality	*Trasler*
IX	Group Problems in Crime and Punishment	*Mannheim*
X	The Institutions of Private Law	*Renner*
XI	Juvenile Delinquency in an English Middletown	*Mannheim*
XII	Legal Aid	*Egerton*
XIII	Pentonville	*Morris and Morris*
XIV	Social Defence	*Ancel*
XV	Young Men in Detention Centres	*Dunlop and McCabe*

LEGAL AID

by

ROBERT EGERTON

With a Preface by

A. L. GOODHART

Routledge
Taylor & Francis Group
LONDON AND NEW YORK

First published in 1945
by Routledge

Reprinted in 1998, 2000, 2002
by Routledge
2 Park Square, Milton Park, Abingdon, Oxon, OX14 4RN
711 Third Avenue, New York, NY 10017

Transferred to Digital Printing 2007

Routledge is an imprint of the Taylor & Francis Group

First issued in paperback 2013

British Library Cataloguing in Publication Data
A CIP catalogue record for this book
is available from the British Library

Legal Aid
978-0-415-17743-6 (hbk)
978-0-415-86391-9 (pbk)
The Sociology of Law and Criminology: 15 Volumes
978-0-415-17832-7
The International Library of Sociology: 274 Volumes
978-0-415-17838-9

Publisher's Note

The publisher has gone to great lengths to ensure the quality of this reprint but points out that some imperfections in the original may be apparent

CONTENTS

PART II. CRITICISM AND PROPOSALS

PREFACE

The Lord Chancellor has recently appointed a committee under the chairmanship of Lord Rushcliffe " to inquire into the present facilities for giving legal advice and assistance to poor persons ", and to make recommendations for " securing that poor persons in need of legal advice may have such facilities at their disposal ". It is unlikely that this committee will have issued its report before this book has been published, but even if it has done so, Mr. Egerton's work will not have lost anything in value for he has included in it much useful information, based on his own experience, which obviously cannot find a place in an official report. He has traced in detail the long and chequered history of legal aid in England, he has described the various systems now in force in other countries, and he has analysed the system, or to be more accurate, the lack of system followed in this country. No one is better qualified than Mr. Egerton to paint an accurate picture of present-day conditions, in view of his experience as Registrar of the Cambridge House (Trinity Hall) Free Legal Advice Centre, which dealt with 4,367 new cases in 1943. Although the large proportion of these were concerned with matrimonial and landlord and tenant disputes in which money claims are rarely at issue, the Centre was able to recover more than £5,000 for applicants. This sum may not seem strikingly large, but when we translate it into human terms and realize that more than 4,000 poor people were given a fair chance to state their cases, we can understand how important this work has been.

For many years social workers have been insisting on the essential importance of providing legal aid for the poor, but it has taken the war to bring the lesson home to those in authority. It is to be hoped that Mr. Egerton's book will also teach this lesson to the general public which is still ignorant of many of the facts. It was the Army which first realized that it was necessary to furnish free legal advice to the soldiers if their morale was not to be affected. As a result, the War Office in July, 1942, produced a scheme for Legal Advice Bureaux, staffed by part-time volunteer solicitors and barristers, and for Command Legal Aid Sections with full-time staff. In November, 1942, the R.A.F. joined in the scheme, and in July, 1943, the Admiralty took similar steps for the Navy. Legal advice by itself was, however, not sufficient; it was also necessary to provide legal aid in the conduct of litigation, especially in matrimonial cases. In 1942, the Law Society therefore set up a department with a salaried staff for conducting divorce cases for poor persons in the Services. By the beginning of 1944 it employed 5 solicitors and a staff of about 60 and included a section for dealing with civilian poor persons' cases.

It was not only in the Services, however, that legal advice was found necessary; the various Citizens' Advice Bureaux, which were established to help civilians with their war-time difficulties, were flooded with questions concerning legal problems. It was difficult to deal with these by voluntary help alone because the amount of work was more than could be dealt with in spare-time hours, so two Legal Advice Centres with salaried staffs have been established in London. It is hardly conceivable that these will be closed after the war, as they have shown how essential this service is to the poor.

Why did we have to wait until the war came before recognizing how serious this problem was? The blame for this must in large part fall on the legal profession, but not for the reasons usually advanced. It is frequently said that the legal profession should have been more ready to give voluntary service to the poor, and that in this regard it compares unfavourably with the medical profession. Mr. Egerton has provided a complete answer to this by showing that the problem is too big a one to be met by voluntary aid. The system established under the Poor Persons' Rules of 1926 has broken down owing to the increasing number of applications, especially since the Matrimonial Causes Act, 1937, came into force. In 1939 there were 10,556 applications of which 5,760 were granted. In 1937 47 per cent. of all divorce suits were brought under the Poor Persons' Rules. As each case represents a minimum contribution of £20 by the conducting solicitor it cannot be said that the legal profession has proved to be ungenerous. To expect solicitors to give voluntary aid in all cases would be as reasonable as to expect doctors to look after their panel patients for nothing. Because poor children need milk is no ground for saying that this should be supplied free by the dairy companies; it is a cost which should fall on the community as a whole.

The legal profession is open to criticism, not because it has been ungenerous, but because it has closed its eyes to a problem which it, in particular, should have recognized. The repetition from time to time of the jest that "the Courts of law, like the Ritz Hotel, are open to the rich and poor alike" showed that some members were aware that the problem existed, but little was done to solve it. Even to-day, as Mr. Egerton has said, "there are still many lawyers who deny the need for the obvious reforms and one may well ask why it is that solicitors and barristers, who ought to be the first to urge the need for professional assistance and who do regularly express their concern at the increasing number of administrative tribunals before which no representation is allowed, oppose the idea of representation for poor persons".

Three reasons for this opposition may be suggested. The first is that the legal profession is still thinking in terms of voluntary legal aid, and that it recognizes that any increase of such aid would be an intolerable burden, especially on those solicitors who have proved to be the most self-sacrificing. The answer to this objection is that no one who has studied the problem believes that voluntary service is the proper basis on which to found a modern system of legal aid. The second reason for the professional opposition is the fear that State control will be introduced if the cost of legal aid is to fall on public funds. Legal aid, it is said, may become bureaucratic. To this it may be answered that bureaucratic legal aid is certainly better than no legal aid at all, but as Mr. Egerton has shown in the final chapters of this book, the danger of bureaucracy can be easily avoided by setting up an independent body, consisting of barristers, solicitors, and social workers, to administer the system. The third objection is the fear that the increase of legal aid will result in the increase of litigation. This is probably true, but it seems odd that lawyers, of all men, should accept the view that litigation is necessarily an evil. Is there not more truth in Dean Pound's statement that "there is danger that in discouraging litigation we encourage wrongdoing"? If a man has a just claim against another, is it not in the public interest that he should be able to assert it in a court of law? The Finlay Committee in its report published in 1928 rejected the idea that legal aid was comparable to medical aid in these words: "It is manifestly in the interests of a State that its citizens should be healthy, not that they should be litigious." But is a poor man who asks for justice in the courts properly described as "litigious"? Is it not more correct to say that it is a paramount interest of a State that its citizens, whether rich or poor, should not be deprived of that justice which Aristotle described as being an essential element of "the good life"?

In this book Mr. Egerton has shown how totally inadequate the present provisions for legal aid are. The result is a sort of crazy patchwork of different ideas and methods. There is one system for criminal law and another for the civil law. There is one system for advice and another for litigation. Strangest of all there is a system of legal aid in the High Court of Justice, but none in the County Courts, where the majority of the cases concerning poor persons would naturally be heard, nor in civil cases before the magistrates. Thus a poor litigant, if he is fortunate, may get legal aid in a petition for divorce, but he must remain unrepresented in a separation and maintenance proceeding, although this may, from the legal standpoint, be far more difficult than an undefended divorce case. To all these various problems Mr. Egerton suggests what to one reader at least seems to be a rational and workable answer. Even if his recommendations are not accepted in full by the Rushcliffe Committee, they deserve the closest study by all those who are interested in one of the most serious problems in our social life.

A. L. GOODHART.

ACKNOWLEDGMENTS

My thanks are due to the following for the generous help they have given in the preparation of this book :

To the Cambridge University Settlement (Cambridge House) for sponsoring the research and report which are incorporated in the following pages.

To many Secretaries of Law Societies, Poor Persons' Committees, Citizens' Advice Bureaux and Social Service organizations for information about legal aid facilities in their areas, and to various informants for information about foreign systems.

To the Trustees and Officials of the British Museum and to the Officials of the Law Society's Library for library facilities.

To J. Mervyn Jones, John Terry and Philip Lawton for reading the manuscript and for many valuable suggestions.

To Professor Goodhart for reading the manuscript and contributing the Preface.

The debt I owe to the authors of various books and articles is acknowledged in the notes to the text where the following abbreviations are used :

L.J.—*Law Journal.*
L.Q.R.—*Law Quarterly Review.*
L.T.—*Law Times.*
S.J.—*Solicitors' Journal.*
J.P.—*Justice of the Peace.*

ROBERT EGERTON.

March 1945.

SHORT BIBLIOGRAPHY

Anyone wishing to make a comprehensive study of Legal Aid should obtain from the National Association of Legal Aid Organizations, New York, "A Tentative Bibliography of Material on Legal Aid Work" compiled by John S. Bradway. A good all-round view of the subject could, however, be obtained by reading the three books and one article first mentioned below.

F. C. G. Gurney-Champion. *Justice and the Poor in England.* (1926.) George Routledge & Sons.

This is a spirited disclosure of the deficiencies in Legal Aid and contains many useful suggestions for remedying them.

Reginald Heber Smith and Bradway. *Growth of Legal Aid Work in the United States.* Dept. of Labor Bulletin No. 607.

An extremely thorough study of the place of Legal Aid in the administration of justice and of the development of this work in America.

J. Mervyn Jones. *Free Legal Advice in England and Wales.* (1940.)

Containing a very valuable study of Poor Man's Lawyer Organizations as well as a short comparative section and suggestions.

E. J. Cohn. *Legal Aid for the Poor.* 59 *L.Q.R.*, 250 and 359.

A discussion, based on a comparative study, of the main points to which attention should be paid in any Legal Aid Scheme.

Other books dealing with Legal Aid are the following:

League of Nations Legal Aid for the Poor. V. Legal 1927, V. 27.

A compilation of reports from many countries as to the Legal Aid facilities existing in those countries.

Reginald Heber Smith. *Justice and the Poor.* (1924.) (3rd Edition.) The Carnegie Foundation, New York.

This American work is the classic on Legal Aid but much of the material is incorporated in the publication of the United States Department of Labor mentioned above.

J. J. Sprigge. *The Shortcomings of the Machinery for Pauper Litigation.* (3rd Edition.) 1893.

A curiously written little book of purely historical interest.

There are also the following books in which Legal Aid is discussed but which are not wholly concerned with the subject:

Sir Edward A. Parry. *The Gospel and the Law.* (1928.)

Claud Mullins. *In Quest of Justice.* (1931.)

"Solicitor." *English Justice.* (1932.) Penguin Edition, 1941.

"A Barrister." *Justice in England.* (1938.) Victor Gollancz.

Richard Meredith Jackson. *The Machinery of Justice in England.* (1940.) Cambridge University Press.

Articles and references to Legal Aid are scattered throughout Legal and other Journals and the following have been selected as being of special interest:

F. W. Blunt. *Law Hospitals: A Suggestion.*

Paper read at the 11th meeting of the Law Society, 1884.

J. P. COLDSTREAM. *The Expediency of Uniformity with regard to Pauper Litigation.* Paper read at the Glasgow Conference of the International Law Association 1901.

J. M. MAGUIRE. *Poverty and Civil Litigation.* 36 Harvard Law Review, 1923, pp. 361 ff., reprinted in 156 *L.T.*, 345–9 and 368–70.
Litigation and Differences of Wealth. 57 *Sol. Jo.*, 419.

P. HARRINGTON EDWARDS. *The Poor and the Law in 1928.* 166 *L.T.*, 233.

J. E. ALLAN-JONES. *Legal Aid for the Poor.* 186 *L.T.*, 296.

S. B. JACOBY. *Legal Aid to the Poor.* Harvard Law Review, 1940, pp. 940 ff.

G. W. KEETON. *Law Reforms after the War.* 50 *L.Q.R.*, 254.

To supplement the valuable historical material in Professor J. M. Maguire's article, the case of Carson *v.* Pickersgill (1885) 54 *L.J.Q.B.*, 484, might be consulted. The Annual Reports of the Law Society record much interesting experience gained in operating the Poor Persons' Procedure. A number of other works are referred to in the text.

The references to the reports of the Departmental Committees mentioned in the text are as follows:
Report of Mr. Justice P. O. Lawrence's Committee, 1921, Cmd. 430.
Report of Mr. Justice P. O. Lawrence's Committee, 1925, Cmd. 2358.
First Report of Mr. Justice Finlay's Committee, 1926, (Criminal), Cmd. 2638.
Final Report of Mr. Justice Finlay's Committee, 1928, Cmd. 3016.
Report of the Poor Person's Representation (Scotland) Committee, 1938, Cmd. 5435.

LEGAL AID

PART I

HISTORICAL AND DESCRIPTIVE

CHAPTER I

INTRODUCTION

At a very early stage in the life of a community it becomes necessary to put a limit on the individual's freedom to do exactly as he likes, and to institute a system of law. The members of a community are encouraged to accept this system and to submit their disputes to an impartial tribunal, instead of "taking the law into their own hands" and endeavouring to gain what they consider their rights by force or subterfuge. Civilized men will voluntarily accept this restraint providing that they can be sure of getting fair and reasonable decisions from the tribunal.

This involves three things: the tribunal must be impartial, it must be accessible, and the laws which it administers must be fair and reasonable. As regards the first of these there is no doubt that a very high standard of impartiality has been attained in the English courts. As regards the last it can be said that there are no laws which directly discriminate between one individual or class and another, and that those which indirectly produce this effect are gradually disappearing as the shape of society alters. It is the second requirement, the one we have labelled "accessibility" which requires further examination.

The laws may be good, the courts may be impartial, but if for any reason the law cannot be invoked, the machinery of justice is of no practical use. Let us consider how this machinery works in the normal case of a man who feels himself injured and entitled to legal redress under English law.

His first step is to consult his solicitor. The solicitor considers the facts of the case, the legal principles and practical considerations involved. He advises his client and, if there appears to be a case, takes the matter up with the opposing party and endeavours to obtain an advantageous settlement. If agreement cannot be reached a Writ or Summons is issued. Faced with the trouble and expense of an action the parties may reconsider their attitudes. If they do not, all the necessary evidence and arguments are collected, a professional advocate on each side tries to show the justice of his case and the fallacies of his opponent's, and the court, having had the benefit of hearing all that has been said for and against each party, decides the matter according to law.

The operation of this machinery is expensive. In addition to the salaries of judges and court officials there are on each side solicitors and barristers, experts and other witnesses, and possibly prolonged investigations and preliminary proceedings, for all of which the litigants have to pay. Obviously there are many people who cannot afford the cost and who, therefore, are not protected by the law unless they are granted special consideration, that is to say, legal aid.

There is no other way in which justice for the poor can be achieved. It is, of course, to be hoped that reforms of, for example, the Workmen's Compensation Acts and Rent Restriction Acts, will reduce the necessity for litigation ; and there are ways, good and bad, in which the expense of legal proceedings can be cut down. The laws can be made simpler, but our complicated economic and social system puts a limit on what can be done in this direction ; the judges and practising lawyers can be less highly trained, but the present tendency in Russia, where this has been tried, is to go in for more legal training ; the procedure of the courts can be of a more summary nature, but it cannot be denied that this involves a lowering of the standard of thoroughness. Everything points to the fact that for many years to come there will continue to be literally millions of citizens who cannot afford to pay for the legal proceedings which are necessary to redress their wrongs and, in so far as the legal aid provided is inadequate, justice is denied to those millions because they are poor.

It is a well-established principle of democracy that all citizens shall enjoy equality before the law, but the practice is more important than the principle. The point has been admirably expressed in a publication of the United States Department of Labor [1] :

[1] Reginald Heber Smith and Bradway : *Growth of Legal Aid Work in the U.S.A.* Dept. of Labor Bulletin, No. 607 (1936), Chap. I. This book is invaluable for a thorough study of legal aid.

> . . . the problem of making justice readily accessible to all, including the great army of wage-earners, is far more than an abstract legalistic controversy. It is a matter of life and death for a democracy because, in the words of Harlan F. Stone, formerly Attorney-General of the United States and now a Justice of the Supreme Court, a democracy " cannot survive if it cannot find a way to make its administration of justice competent ". In similar vein Mr. Chief Justice Hughes says : " It is idle to speak of the blessings of liberty unless the poor enjoy the equal protection of the laws."
>
> Lord Shaw, in his address to the American Bar Association in 1922, stated the point without quibble or evasion when he said : " That society is rotten where one citizen as against another can overpower him or undermine him by law wielded with an uneven hand. Only the blind, cruel, or the unjust in heart can wink the eye at this unnameable curse."

In this, as in practically every other civilized country, the most obvious hardships have been mitigated by the introduction of legal aid, but the provisions have been introduced piecemeal, so that there is one system for poor prisoners and a different one for poor litigants in the High Court ; legal advice, as distinct from assistance with litigation, has been left entirely to charitable effort ; some aspects of the problem have not been dealt with at all and many reforms are long overdue.

The problem is not small, or unimportant. In 1941–2 only about 9,000,000 people in England and Wales were paying any income tax ; in 1938–9, just over 3,500,000. The remainder of the forty-one and a half million do not all require legal aid, because some of them are wives with husbands, or children with parents, who can afford to pay for legal services for their dependants, but the numbers involved are very substantial and there are many people who are at present unable to enforce their rights by legal process.

The public has become resigned to this state of affairs, partly because the law tends to be something of a mystery to the layman and partly because each individual only comes into contact with it on rare occasions. The need for legal services has, however, grown enormously during this century and is still growing. More social legislation has been passed affecting the poorer classes and practically every activity is governed by laws and regulations. At the same time our conception of the rights of the ordinary man has been enlarged.

The administration of justice has not kept pace with the growing enthusiasm for making democracy a reality.

Roscoe Pound, Dean of the Harvard Law School [1] says:

> It is so obvious that we have almost ceased to remark it, that in petty causes—that is, with respect to the everyday rights and wrongs of the great majority of the urban community—the machinery whereby rights are secured practically defeats rights by making it impracticable to assert them when they are infringed. Moreover, there is danger that in discouraging litigation we encourage wrongdoing, and it requires very little experience in the legal aid societies in any of our cities to teach us that we have been doing that very thing.

Experience in this country leads to the same conclusion: the impossibility of paying for a divorce leads to unmarried couples, illegitimate children and bigamy, the difficulty of obtaining redress is responsible for many cases of assault, wrongful seizure of goods and many forms of anti-social behaviour. It has been found in the United States [2] that the absence of legal aid is one of the principal causes of industrial unrest and in this connection it is interesting to note that Sir William Beveridge puts first amongst the disadvantages of the Workmen's Compensation Acts [3] the fact that they rest in the last resort upon the threat or the practice of litigation and that no machinery exists for assisting the employee in presenting his claim, with the result that he often suspects injustice.

Even more serious consequences are hinted at in the book *English Justice* by "Solicitor", where it is said that "It should be unnecessary to emphasize the importance of confidence in the administration of justice. This confidence has made our revolutions comparatively bloodless." [4] . . . While it would be absurd to fear bloody revolution in the cause of legal aid there is reason for serious discontent. It is a fact that a lawyer often has to say to a poor client, "You have a legal right, but in practice you can do nothing about it because you have not the money." That position inevitably causes suffering and hardship to the poor and, accompanied by a sense of injustice, it breeds bitterness and contempt for democratic institutions and for the law.

No doubt absolute equality in the administration of justice is a dream. Even leaving aside superiority of brains and education, the man who can afford to pay for the very best counsel and to provide against every possible contingency, without counting the cost, will have the advantage. Litigation is still "trial by battle under another form; counsel being the champions and purses

[1] *The Spirit of the Common Law*; quoted by Smith and Bradway, op. cit.
[2] Manley Report of the U.S. Commission on Industrial Relations.
[3] *Social Insurance and Allied Services*, Cmd. 6404, para. 79. [4] Preface.

the weapons ". Yet it is surely not putting the case too high to say that every citizen of a democracy should be in a position to take all reasonable and prudent steps which may be necessary to safeguard his legal rights.

In this sense equality before the law can easily be attained. The problem arises from the poverty (compared with legal costs) of a large section of the population, and it can be solved by money. There is sufficient truth in this statement by the most outspoken of the critics of our legal aid system to make it sting : " One of the unacknowledged reasons," says " Barrister," " for restricting the facilities for poor men's litigation is that, if they were really given adequate means for enforcing their rights or defending themselves against injustice, the courts would be choked with a huge volume of additional work, at an expense which the governing class is unwilling to face." [1] Actually there is no reason why the amount of litigation should be enormously increased or why the cost of adequate measures should be more than a minute fraction of the national expenditure on social services. The real enemies of reform are apathy and the conservatism of the legal profession.

In the following chapters the English provisions relating to legal aid, past and present, are described, particulars are given of the arrangements in other countries, and subsequently the matters which require reform are pointed out and various proposals for reform are discussed. Although there may be differences of opinion as to the best organisation to secure the desired end, it is thought that there will be little disagreement, except in detail, with the nature of the reforms that are advocated.

It was said long ago that " the amendment of the law has suffered greatly from the circumstance of its being generally supposed that the subject belongs to lawyers exclusively." [2] Legal aid in particular is a matter to which social workers and others can make a great contribution. The interests of lawyers are too closely involved for them to take an entirely unprejudiced view of the situation and it is difficult to convince them that the extension of legal services to the whole population is not only their duty but is also to their advantage. It cannot be expected that the law will escape the searching scrutiny to which all the other aspects of our social system are being submitted. The process has in fact already begun. Legal aid reform will come ; it is only a question of how soon, and how thorough it will be.

[1] " Barrister " : *Justice in England* (1938).

[2] Lord Westbury, 1863.

CHAPTER II

THE POOR IN THE COURTS BEFORE 1914 [1]

In the earliest days of legal procedure we find small concessions being made to overcome the disadvantages of the poor. In the reign of Henry Ist the requirement that security must be given by a suitor was qualified by a provision " that those who had not sufficient present security should pledge their faith to make satisfaction to the utmost of their powers ". Another early concession was that ecclesiastical lawyers, who between the ninth and thirteenth centuries were prohibited from practising in the temporal courts in ordinary cases were customarily allowed to do so on behalf of the poor. It is hardly likely however that the assistance given was any greater than at the somewhat later date when Piers Plowman complained of the lawyers of his day—

> " Thou mightest better mete the mist on Malvern hills
> Than get a mutter from their mouths save thou show thy money."

In Magna Carta the principle is laid down on which the whole claim for legal aid might reasonably be based.

> " To no man will we deny, to no man will we sell,
> or delay, justice or right."

This general statement, incorporated in the United States Constitution has, in fact, been held by the courts of some States to give them power to grant legal aid where no specific provisions exist. And Gurney Champion, the author of *Justice and the Poor in England*, felt so strongly that the promise was no longer being honoured that he printed, as an Appendix to his book, a Draft Bill to repeal this section of Magna Carta " in so far only as poor persons are concerned ". This, he maintained should, for the sake of honesty, be passed by Parliament unless it was willing to increase the legal assistance given to the poor.

In the reign of Henry III (1216–1272) the Common Law courts had power to issue writs and hear the cases of needy suitors without fees, but from 1278, when the Statutes requiring costs to be awarded came into force, the relief which could be given in the courts, except the Ecclesiastical Courts which had an

[1] For much of the material in this chapter I am indebted to Professor Maguire's article *Poverty and Civil Litigation*, 36 Harvard Law Review (1923), pp. 361 ff., reprinted in 156 *L.T.*, 345–9, 368–70.

in forma pauperis procedure of their own, was very limited. The King's Prerogative was, however, frequently exercised in order to remove injustice arising from poverty, and the Justices of Eyre, who travelled through the country for the purpose of clearing up all outstanding legal business, received many appeals from paupers and by their informal procedure were able to deal with cases which could never have been brought in the ordinary courts. This exercise of the Prerogative was continued in the early practice of the Chancery Courts, including the Star Chamber and the Court of Requests.

In 1494 we get the first Statute dealing specifically with *in forma pauperis* procedure, 11 Henry VII c. 12:

> "Every poor person . . . shall have . . . writ or writs . . . according to the nature of their causes, therefor paying nothing to your Highness for the seals of the same, nor to any person for the writing of the same writ or writs ; . . . and that the Lord Chancellor shall assign . . . learned counsel and attorneys for the same without any reward taking thereof; and . . . the Justices shall assign to the same poor person or persons counsel learned by their discretion, which shall give their counsel nothing taking for the same ; and likewise the Justices shall appoint attorney and attorneys for the same poor person or persons, and all other officers requisite, . . . which shall do their duties without any reward for their counsel, help and business in the same."

The surprisingly comprehensive nature of this Statute was only marred by the fact that it did not apply to defendants and in the Common Law courts this defect was not remedied until 1883.

In 1531 a further enactment is passed, 23 Henry VIII c. 15, providing that a poor person, if unsuccessful shall not be liable for his opponents' costs, but for such "other punysshement as shall be thought reasonable". The nature of this "other punysshement" is indicated by the form of order for admitting a plaintiff to sue *in forma pauperis* which was in use during the reign of Elizabeth : "But if the matter shall fall out against the Plaintiff, he shall be punished with whipping and pillory", and, although it has been doubted whether the order was ever put into effect, Professor Maguire states that there is a very specific account of a flogging having occurred.

This crude attempt to prevent vexatious litigation points to the weakness of the otherwise excellent legislation. Applications for the benefit of the procedure were made in open court and there was no machinery for investigating the means of the applicant and the merits of the case, and thus safeguarding the courts and the opposing party in the suit.

The number of vexatious cases which were commenced brought the system into disrepute and resulted in a tightening up in the attitude of the courts. An indication of the dissatisfaction which was felt with these pauper suits is the fact that in 1653 the committee of the "Barebones Parliament" tried to revive the system of "other punysshement" proposing that "when any person is admitted to sue as a poor man and shall appeal, and the same shall be adjudged causeless, he shall be sent to the work-house, to continue there a month and also be whipped".

By 1774 a Counsel's certificate as to the merits of the case was necessary before the benefit of *in forma pauperis* procedure could be obtained, and about 1786 fees of £4 or over had to be paid in some cases before the poor person could recover a penny of the judgment which had been awarded to him. The theory was that a person who was awarded judgment for more than £5 thereby ceased to be a pauper, and on this same theory an improper practice grew up of counsel and attorneys claiming fees, if successful, from the poor person, who then claimed costs from his opponent.

In the Chancery Courts there was nothing to prevent the opponent being made liable for the pauper's costs since the Statutes did not apply to these courts and were adopted only so far as seemed equitable. The practice differed in other respects. Defendants, as well as plaintiffs, could proceed *in forma pauperis* in the Chancery Court, on the other hand, until 1774, and possibly later, no appeal was allowed in Chancery in *in forma pauperis* cases; Lord Eldon thought "it was a very singular proposition, and he could not see why, because a party was poor, the Court should not set itself right". The practice of charging costs was stopped, so far as the Common Law courts were concerned, in 1853, and soon afterwards the Chancery procedure was brought into line with Common Law procedure.

In 1883 the statute of Henry VII was repealed by the Statute Law Revision Act, and Rules of Court were passed regulating the *in forma pauperis* procedure in the High Court. The applicant now had to be worth not more than £25, instead of £5, as before, and applications had to be supported by an Opinion of Counsel as to the reasonableness of the proceedings and an affidavit of the applicant or his solicitor. The poor person thus had to find a solicitor who would prepare his Case to Counsel and Affidavit, and a Counsel who would give an Opinion ; and, as the solicitor and Counsel who did these kindnesses were likely to be chosen by the Court to conduct the case free of charge, it was bound to be extremely difficult for a poor suitor even to present his application. The procedure became almost inoperative * and the conditions attached to it were described by *The Times* [1] as " prohibitive ". In 1912 and 1913 there was considerable agitation for reform and shortly afterwards a new scheme was introduced which provided the foundation for the modern practice.

* In 1914 there were only 99 Petitions presented by Poor Persons ; R. M. Jackson, *The Machinery of Justice in England.*

[1] Leading article in *The Times*, 30th December, 1912.

CHAPTER III

POOR PERSONS' PROCEDURE 1914–44

There were two main factors which brought about the new set of rules governing what became known as Poor Persons' Procedure. The first, and probably less weighty, was the growth from 1890 onwards of Poor Man's Lawyers, described in the next chapter. The lawyers and social workers concerned in these charitable ventures came directly into contact with the distress and injustice caused to the poorer classes by their inability to enforce their legal rights in the courts and constituted a small body of people who were able to urge the redress of these wrongs in an articulate manner. The second factor was the scandal of "ambulance-chasing". The poor, for whom the Rules of 1883 provided no adequate remedy, had become the prey of unscrupulous lawyers and others, who would take up their cases in the hope of recovering costs from the other side. This was the subject of a long letter to *The Times* from Sir John Collie in December 1912,[1] which was followed by a letter from a Poor Man's Lawyer [2] pointing out that until better provision was made these spurious Legal Aid Societies and Speculative Solicitors were a necessary evil.

Judge Parry [3] gives another cause for the new measures, namely, the determination of the divorce court practitioners to preserve their lucrative practices which were threatened by the possibility of divorce business being transferred to the County Courts unless a way could be found for assisting the thousands of people who were seeking divorces but were unable to pay the cost. However this may be the Bar, and particularly the Divorce Court practitioners, were wholly obstructive when the new Rules were first issued.[4] They objected to the proposals on the grounds that they involved too heavy a burden on the Bar and also that, in providing for the payment of counsel by the poor person's opponent, if unsuccessful, they infringed the "primary rule of Bar morality" that payment of counsel should not be affected by the result of a case.

[1] *The Times*, 27th December, 1912.

[2] *The Times*, 30th December, 1912. The correspondence was continued on 3rd and 7th January, 1913, and there were editorial comments on 30th December, 1912, 18th March, 1913, and 5th June, 1913.

[3] *The Gospel and the Law* (1928).

[4] 47 *Law Journal* (1912), p. 48, and 48 *L.J.*, 468.

The Law Society was hardly more enthusiastic but passed a resolution that " in view of the evident trend of public opinion in favour of aiding poor persons unable to procure legal advice and assistance through the ordinary channels, and in view of the frequent cases in which such persons are victimized by so-called Legal Aid Societies—and by other means—with which certain solicitors are associated . . . desirable that the Law Society should . . . show interest, etc ".[1]

For a time it looked as though a solution might be found in an extension of the charitable Poor Man's Lawyer organizations.[2] The Law Society called a conference at which a constitution and regulations for a " Poor Man's Lawyer Association of London " were drawn up and these were later approved by the Law Society. But the Association was apparently never formed and the new Poor Persons' Rules which came into force in June 1914 made no provision for the giving of advice.

With these Rules the framework of the present Poor Persons' Procedure was brought into being. They covered only proceedings in the High Court and Court of Appeal. Administration was in the hands of " prescribed officers ", constituting the Poor Persons' Department. Applications were made to a Master of the Supreme Court and were referred by him to unpaid " reporters ", consisting of barristers and solicitors. The report was presented to the court, which then gave its decision on the application and, if a certificate was granted, volunteers from both branches of the legal profession conducted the case free of charge and court fees were remitted. Certificates could only be granted to applicants who were not worth £50, " or such larger sum not exceeding £100 as a Judge personally under special circumstances may direct ". It was originally intended that a Treasury fund should be set up, out of which the out-of-pocket expenses of a case, such as travelling expenses of witnesses, should be defrayed when necessary.[3] This did not materialize and, as an alternative a committee was to be formed, with the Lord Chancellor's blessing, to appeal to the public for contributions for this purpose.[4] The war came in 1914 and nothing more was ever done.

The scheme was welcomed by *The Times* and the *Law Journal*, and Dr. W. R. Bisschop, Secretary of the Central Legal Aid

[1] Annual Report, 1913.
[2] Annual Reports, 1913 and 1914; 48 *L.J.*, 180 and 288; 57 *S.J.*, 383.
[3] Annual Report, 1914; 48 *L.J.*, 468. [4] 49 *L.J.*, 468.

Society, wrote: "A serious attempt is being made to re-open to the poor the doors of the Law Courts, which have been practically closed to them ever since 1883."[1] But the Law Society disapproved of the "officialism" of the Poor Persons' Department and, if it is not true to say that solicitors sabotaged the Department, they are only exonerated on the principle of the legal tag,

> Thou shalt not kill, but need'st not strive
> Officiously to keep alive.

No mention of a poor person is made in the Law Society's Reports from 1915 to 1920. In 1919 the system was working so badly that Lord Birkenhead found it necessary to appoint a committee under Mr. Justice P. O. Lawrence to report on the working of the Poor Persons' Rules.

The first point which emerged from the committee's report[2] was that virtually only matrimonial cases were being dealt with; in 1918 the number of certificates for other types of cases was 78 The figures for the matrimonial cases are in themselves striking:

Applications made	Applications granted	Petitions filed	Cases heard	Successful cases
4,101	2,215	1,014	486	471

Of the applications granted 2,120 were by Petitioners, less than one-half of this number filed Petitions and less than one-half of the number of Petitions filed was carried to a hearing. "We have found," reported the Committee, "that [this great discrepancy] is mainly due to the Poor Persons being unable to find the necessary out-of-pocket expenses to enable them to start or to proceed with their cases."

After stating that out-of-pockets in an ordinary case amounted to £5, chiefly for travelling expenses of witnesses, office expenses amounted to a further £5, and that in nullity cases the total was £25, the Report continued:

"Unless a fund is constituted out of which the expenses of the Poor Persons can be defrayed, the really poor or quite destitute persons have no chance of availing themselves of the Rules to obtain a divorce."

One would have thought that this would have led the Committee to recommend the setting up of such a fund, as had been contemplated when the Rules were issued, but there was another consideration: only, or, as the Committee said, at least, 68

[1] *The Times*, 5th June, 1913; 49 *L.J.*, 362; 48 *L.J.*, 242. [2] Cmd. 430.

solicitors in London undertook Poor Persons' Matrimonial cases in 1918, as compared with 790 who undertook them for their own clients or as agents, and of these 68 some were making a business out of it. One solicitor had taken 401 Poor Persons' cases in a single year:

> A practice has sprung up amongst the conducting solicitors of demanding (as a first step, after they have been assigned) a sum of money from the Poor Person to cover out-of-pocket expenses.
>
> The Taxing Officers in the Probate and Divorce Division allow a sum for "office expenses", in addition to actual out-of-pocket expenses, with the result that some of the solicitors who now undertake a large number of these cases have engaged special clerks for this purpose, and carry on a remunerative practice in Poor Persons' cases.
>
> If the money demanded from the Poor Persons is not forthcoming, nothing is done; if the money is sent, the case is proceeded with, until, in the opinion of the solicitors, it is exhausted by out-of-pocket and "office expenses". When this occurs more money is asked for; if it is not forthcoming, the case stops; if more is sent, the case proceeds as before.

Evidently the necessity of stopping solicitors receiving a sum for office expenses, allowed by the Taxing Masters, appeared to the Committee of paramount importance. Admittedly "it may result in nobody being found willing to undertake these cases", but the solution to that was to reduce the number of cases by requiring Poor Persons to make a deposit, of £5 in divorce and £20 in nullity cases, which many of them could not find.

> If a fund were established to provide for the expenses of Poor Persons' cases, a wholly different state of things would arise and the number of applications, as well as of cases entered and tried, would no doubt increase enormously.
>
> It would, in our opinion, be essential in that case to give some profit costs which in turn would probably lead to speculative solicitors hunting up cases.

The Report secured the abolition of "office expenses", payment to the Poor Persons' Department of a deposit for out-of-pocket expenses at the time of making the application, and the addition of an income test of £2 a week, or, in special circumstances, £4 a week, to the existing capital test.

The result of these amendments is described in the Report of a Special Committee of the Law Society which was presented to the Council in March 1923.[1]

[1] Figures relating to applications by Poor Persons will be found in Appendix C.

The new Rules came into force on 1st January, 1921, and the Council of the Law Society made an appeal to all solicitors to take Poor Persons' cases. The result was:

In London	334	solicitors undertook to conduct	698 cases
In the provinces	1,383	solicitors undertook to conduct	2,838 cases
	1,717		3,536

This sufficed till May 1922, when solicitors in London for a further 200 cases were needed. A further appeal was made and 123 solicitors in London offered to conduct 251 cases.

On the 5th September, 1922, there were only sufficient solicitors to deal with about 35 London cases before the end of the year; there were 1,400 cases in the office and applications were being granted at the rate of 90 per month.

On 25th October, 1922, as a result of withdrawals, there were only 313 London solicitors on the rota, with a nominal capacity of 754 cases, practically all of which had been taken. The President therefore made a further appeal to every London and provincial solicitor. In London 68 new solicitors and 32 existing solicitors offered to provide representation in a further 227 divorce, and 10 other, cases. In the provinces 229 new and 58 existing solicitors offered to take 818 more cases.

In the provinces more than enough solicitors would have been available, if they had been equally distributed, but assistance was greatly needed in 17 towns or counties.

Although the number of certificates granted had been cut by nearly half, and although after all these efforts had been made the Council had to admit that a breakdown of the system was imminent, they still agreed with the Lawrence Committee that "any system that will allow a profit to be made out of these cases is liable to abuse and would not be satisfactory". The only recommendations which the Law Society's special committee could make were that more divorce work should be dealt with in the provinces and that the State should provide a fund for out-of-pocket expenses in cases where these amounted to more than £5. The Report of this special committee was justly described by the *Justice of the Peace* as only a palliation, yet solicitors still took little interest in the fact that the one official attempt to provide legal services for a large section of the population had broken down—"After a very brief discussion, in which a few points of detail were raised by members . . . this motion [the adoption of the

Report] was put to the meeting and carried by a majority of six to one." [1]

The result was that in July 1923 the Lord Chancellor appointed another Committee, again under Mr. Justice Lawrence. Shortly afterwards Sir Claude Schuster echoed the warning,[2] already given in the Lawrence Report and in the columns of the *Justice of the Peace* [3] that, if the solicitors' profession did not deal with the problem, a Government department would have to be considered. During the following year, while the broken-down Poor Persons' Procedure staggered along waiting for the Lawrence Committee's further report, which had been held up by the General Elections, the *Law Journal* took the opportunity of discussing the matter from several angles, describing it as " one of the most important—indeed, we think we should properly say, the most important—of the questions with which the profession is faced . . . the matter is one profoundly affecting the relations of the profession both with the State and with the public.[4]

When the second Lawrence Report [5] was presented in February 1925 it was found to be concerned solely with the shortage of conducting solicitors. Although the number of matrimonial applications granted had dropped from 2,215 in 1918 to 1,254 in 1924 the number of Petitions filed was still only just over half the number of successful applicants, but this was not considered a " difficulty ".—" The difficulties which have arisen in the working of the Poor Persons' Rules have been caused solely by reason of the inability of the Poor Persons' Department to find an adequate number of solicitors willing to undertake the conduct of the large number of divorce cases brought by and against poor persons."

The solution adopted arose from a very simple line of reasoning : there is a certain amount of voluntary effort available which it would be stupid to waste ; therefore the services of lawyers should remain gratuitous. A gratuitous system depends upon the goodwill of solicitors therefore the demands of solicitors must be met. These were : more decentralization of divorce work, a Government grant towards administration expenses, and control of the scheme.

Having regard, no doubt, to the apparently small number of cases involved, the proposals were received with approval. In addition to the measures which had been proposed the Law

[1] 87 *J.P.*, 305 and 350. [2] 68 *S.J.*, 97. [3] 87 *J.P.*, 86.
[4] 59 *L.J.*, 720, 767 ; 60 *L.J.*, 136, 213, 237, 261. [5] Cmd. 2358.

Society rightly insisted that a central office was needed and took over the office and staff of the old Poor Persons' Department.[1] From now on the Law Societies are in sole control. Not only do committees appointed by them receive and investigate the applications for aid but they grant or refuse applications in the place of the court. The State's responsibility is confined to the payment of a few thousand pounds a year for administration expenses and the sacrifice of court fees.

Over 80 Poor Persons' Committees of the London and Provincial Law Societies were set up ; Swansea and some other areas were not covered for a time, but eventually the organization was completed.[2] In some districts practically every solicitor volunteered to conduct one or more cases, in others some difficulty was encountered. London solicitors were the least responsive ; out of over 5,000 practising solicitors, in 1927 only 580 solicitors were on the rota, with a capacity for 1,101 cases, but by persistent efforts, constantly pressing for the conduct of more divorce work in the provinces and encouraging provincial solicitors who did not normally do divorce work to take poor persons' cases, the arrears were at once greatly reduced. There were 1,599 applications pending at the beginning of 1926, 624 at the beginning of 1927.[3]

The numbers grew every year and after 1937 when the Matrimonial Causes Act came into force there was a large and permanent rise in the amount of business to be dealt with. Indeed some committees were stated to be still in arrears in 1943 as a result of the flood of cases which followed on this Act. In 1929 the applications made were 4,817 ; in 1939, 10,556. Applications granted in the same years were 2,315 and 5,760 respectively. The Treasury support, which consisted of the provision of accommodation and an annual grant which was as low as £3,000 at one time, reached £11,000 for 1943–4. The rest of the burden, and it was very considerable, was borne by the legal profession, or rather by that section of it which volunteered to take poor persons' cases. Sir John Withers estimated[4] that an average undefended divorce suit represented a contribution of £20 by the conducting solicitor, and in 1937 47 per cent. of all divorce suits heard by the courts were poor persons' cases. Defended and complicated cases were, of course, more expensive. A case is reported, which is by no means an isolated instance, where the solicitors' bill would have come to

[1] Annual Report, 1926.
[2] 160 *Law Times*, 60.
[3] Annual Report, 1928.
[4] 165 *L.T.*, 402.

£200.[1] The work done by the honorary secretaries of Poor Persons' Committees, who, in practice, had to help with applications and advice, as well as their committee work, was enormous. There was never a shortage of barristers, except in a few areas, though it may be doubted whether they were always " learned by their discretion ". Until 1942 the whole of the High Court work for poor persons, apart from speculative litigation, was carried out by the organized charity of the legal profession. Even when the poor person was successful against a rich opponent his lawyers were not entitled as a rule to receive payment.

The burden of Poor Persons' Procedure was naturally most felt in those areas where there was a high proportion of poor people and in 1939 the Associated Law Societies of Wales passed resolutions [2] that they and their Poor Persons' Committees would not deal with any Poor Persons' cases after June 1939 until the following reforms were granted :

1. A reasonable fee was paid to the conducting solicitor.
2. General jurisdiction in Divorce was extended to every Assize and District Registry.
3. The non-liability for costs of a Poor Persons' opponent was removed.

The Council of the Law Society replied strongly deprecating the threat and stating that it would in no circumstances agree to the first proposal ; it would not cease in its efforts to secure the second and it would consider the third. Later the third proposal was approved and rules were drafted to cover the point, but in spite of a further appeal for co-operation all the Welsh Law Societies with the exception of Merthyr and Aberdare refused to rescind their decision.[3]

The war brought a fresh and overwhelming crisis in the affairs of the Poor Persons' Committees. The call-up of solicitors and their clerks threw more work on to the shoulders of the older men who remained and the voluntary work on which Poor Persons' procedure depended was bound to be the first to suffer. The number of solicitors on the rotas was reduced by over 50 per cent. In London there were 857 solicitors on the rota in 1938 and 350 in 1943 and the figures for Counsel were 602 and 110. A large decrease in the number of applications might have been expected since there was far more employment and higher wages, while the means test remained the same, but this was not the case. Already

[1] Annual Report, 1934. [2] Annual Report, 1939.
[3] Annual Report, 1941.

in 1940 the London Committee had 600 divorce cases for which certificates had been granted and deposits paid but for which no conducting solicitors could be found. In some areas applicants had to wait two years or more before a start could be made on their cases. Several Committees simply decided that they would grant no more applications for the duration. The total number of Poor Persons' cases commenced in 1940 decreased by 1,185 to 2,739.

This state of affairs might have gone unremedied on the ground of emergency conditions but for one paramount consideration—the morale of the fighting Forces, which was severely affected, as was that of civilians, by anxiety over their personal affairs. Only a drastic solution could deal with the accumulated and growing number of cases and on 1st January, 1942, a Department of the Law Society began to operate, not simply as an administrative Department, but actually conducting divorce cases in the place of firms of solicitors. The formation and growth of the Department were described in the address of the President of the Law Society on 28th January, 1944:

. . . indeed, some two or three years ago the Procedure was in imminent danger of a breakdown by reason of the acute shortage of solicitors and experienced clerks remaining to continue its administration. The Council, however, did everything that in them lay to relieve this situation, and with that object at the beginning of 1942 we set up a department in this building called the Services Divorce Department, to conduct any matrimonial cause in the High Court under the Poor Persons Procedure, where any of the parties to such cause is in the Services. That step was taken after representations received from the authorities of their urgent desire that men and women on service should be relieved from anxiety in respect of their domestic affairs. The Department as at first formed consisted of one solicitor, one managing clerk and a few typists. This staff was subsequently increased until 13 clerks were employed. Later the flood of cases was such that we engaged another solicitor, with 13 additional clerks, and we have recently added two more solicitors with an even further increased staff. The Provincial Committees are thus relieved by the knowledge that they can assign to the London Committee any Service case with which they cannot deal locally. Notwithstanding all this, we learned that a number of Committees were still unable to find solicitors to conduct cases where all the parties were civilians. The Council accordingly decided to add once again to our Department here by the creation of a civilian section with a fifth solicitor and staff for the conduct of matrimonial cases in respect of which local Committees may find themselves in difficulty. Thirty-four Poor Persons Committees have taken advantage of the facilities afforded by the civilian section, and we are glad to have been able to relieve them. It is indeed for that reason that many Committees have reported that they are abreast of their work.

No less than 5,521 Service cases have been assigned to the Department, and 1,065 civilian cases since the civilian section was established. The Department, as a whole, have filed 3,316 petitions, 1,643 cases have been set down, and 1,113 decrees nisi have been obtained.

The organization of the Department, which now numbers some 60 persons has been difficult.

The Department is helped by the legal advice system set up by the War Office in the course of 1942, on the other hand it is hampered by the large amount of work which has to be done by correspondence and by the delay which is caused by the movement of troops. Applicants are still required to pay deposits of £5 and sometimes more ; out of these the Law Society is entitled to claim 3 guineas for the expenses of the Department. It is something of a revelation to find that, when the Department is working at full efficiency, it is expected that it will be entirely self-supporting on these payments of 3 guineas by each applicant.[1]

To serving men and women, and those who wished to bring petitions against members of the Services, as also to civilians since the scheme was extended to them, the Department has been of enormous service and its success is bound to have a profound effect on future developments.

[1] See the President's statement at the Annual General Meeting of the Law Society on 7th July, 1944.

CHAPTER IV

PROCEEDINGS IN OTHER COURTS

The Poor Persons' Rules, it must be stated again—for even lawyers are sometimes ignorant of the fact—apply only to proceedings in the High Court, so that proceedings in the House of Lords, the Privy Council, the Criminal Courts, the County Courts, and so-called quasi-civil cases in the Police Courts, are all either governed by a different set of rules or not provided with legal aid at all.

House of Lords

In the House of Lords an appellant or respondent can be granted leave to plead *in forma pauperis* and is then relieved from paying the fees of the House and from giving security for costs ; he cannot be made liable for his opponent's costs if the appeal fails, while if it is successful, he can recover his solicitor's out-of-pocket expenses plus three-eighths of the profit costs, excluding fees of counsel. No representation is provided and no assistance is given to enable the pauper to pay out-of-pocket expenses.

Criminal Courts

In the criminal courts a person accused of a crime who could not afford to pay the normal fees was originally dependent upon the system of " dock briefs ". This was a custom of the Bar whereby the Judge, if he thought it necessary, could call upon any barrister who was in court and gowned, to undertake the prisoner's defence free of charge. If the prisoner could produce £1 3*s.* 6*d.* in court he was himself entitled to select the barrister to act for him.

This professional obligation was sometimes evaded and sometimes accepted with bad grace.* The counsel who were anxious to take these cases were, for the most part, barristers who, owing to inexperience or some other reason, had not been entrusted by solicitors with more remunerative work, and who hoped to attract notice by their conduct of the defence. Unfortunately it was

* Incidents are reported in the newspapers from time to time. The *News Chronicle* of 14th April, 1944, reported Mr. J. H. Thorpe, K.C., deputy chairman, as saying at Middlesex Sessions : " The general scuttle of counsel to get out of court when a prisoner expresses a wish from the dock to be represented is neither seemly nor in the public interest."

sometimes the wrong kind of notice as in the case of the old lag, who after having had the doubtful benefit of a dock brief and been convicted, was asked whether he had anything to say before sentence and replied, "Nothing, my Lord, except to plead the youth and inexperience of my counsel." Even if the barrister was competent and willing, he was required to do all the work which would normally be done for him by a solicitor; he had only a short time in which to find out the facts of the case and no opportunity of producing the necessary witnesses or preparing the defence in a proper manner.

The "dock brief" system is still sometimes used even now, although it was largely replaced by the *Poor Prisoners' Defence Act*, 1903, and this Act was in turn revised in 1930 as a result of recommendations made in the first Report [1] of the Committee on Legal Aid, appointed in 1925 by the Lord Chancellor and the Home Secretary jointly to enquire into the facilities for legal advice and legal assistance other than the matters covered by the Poor Persons' Rules.

The *Poor Prisoners' Defence Act*, 1930, provides that any person committed for trial for an indictable offence may apply, either to a Police Court or to the trial court, for a *defence certificate*. If "his means are insufficient to enable him to obtain" legal aid the certificate is granted, as of right, if the charge is murder, and is granted in other cases if it is considered "desirable in the interests of justice".

In addition to this provision for trials at Quarter Sessions and Assizes, the same Act gives a Police Court power to grant a *legal aid certificate* if the Court considers "that by reason of the gravity of the charge or of exceptional circumstances it is desirable in the interests of justice that he should have legal aid before them". The section, it will be seen, covers both cases tried by magistrates and preliminary examinations before magistrates.

A *defence certificate* entitles the prisoner to a solicitor and counsel and a copy of the depositions. Under a legal aid certificate it is usual for a solicitor only to be assigned, but in murder cases counsel may also be assigned if the magistrates think fit; an allowance may also be made of "any other expenses properly incurred in carrying on the defence". The cost is borne by local funds. Under a *legal aid certificate* solicitors receive 3 guineas and counsel £3 5*s*. 6*d*. Under a *defence certificate* and an *appeal aid certificate* (mentioned below) the fees are on the following scale,

[1] Cmd. 2638.

varying according to whether or not the case is of exceptional length or difficulty: solicitor, 4 guineas to £9; junior counsel, £3 5*s.* 6*d.* to £11; senior counsel, £5 10*s.* to £16 5*s.*

The 1926 Report dealt with the question of appeals from the police courts in a somewhat surprising manner.[1] It pointed out that an appellant was required to enter into recognizance, with or without sureties, to pay the costs of the appeal if ordered. This, the Committee thought, made legal aid unnecessary since "the appellant, having entered into the recognizances, can probably afford to pay his own costs, and the position of the respondent is sufficiently secured by the fact that the recognizances have been entered into". It appears to have been recognized that this argument was fallacious since provision was, after a decent interval, made for legal aid for appeals from police courts by the *Summary Jurisdiction (Appeals) Act*, 1933. Any appellant or respondent who has not sufficient means to enable him to obtain legal assistance in connection with the appeal may apply to a police court for an *appeal aid certificate*. It is to be granted if "by reason of the nature of the offence of which the appellant was convicted, or by reason of the sentence, or of exceptional circumstances, it is desirable in the interests of justice". The Rules made under this Act allow the solicitor to receive, in addition to the prescribed fees, his travelling expenses and "any other out-of-pocket expenses actually and reasonably incurred".

By the *Criminal Appeal Act*, 1907, legal aid must, in murder appeals, and may, in other cases, be granted for appeals to the Court of Criminal Appeal.

Civil Police Court Cases

In addition to criminal jurisdiction, the Police Courts deal with a considerable number of quasi-civil cases, particularly separation and maintenance and affiliation cases, but, although it was recommended in the 1926 Report,[2] no legal aid is provided for these cases apart from the general power, which the Police Court has to dispense with payment of the few shillings which are normally charged for a Summons or other proceedings.

County Courts

Not even this amount of assistance is provided in the County Courts, where fees, although much higher than those of the Police

[1] Cmd. 2638, para. 18. [2] Para. 17.

Court, cannot be remitted, and representation cannot be provided, except in the relatively few cases which have been commenced in the High Court. Strangely enough this does not seem to have been decided until 1922, for in 1849, in Chinn *v.* Bullen,[1] it was held that section 78 of the *County Court Act*, which said that where no express provision was made in the Act the general principles of practice of the superior courts were to be followed, entitled the County Court to permit proceedings *in forma pauperis* as in the High Court. It is not known how generally this practice was followed but in 1912 the *Law Journal* mentions *in forma pauperis* procedure in the County Court [2] and no precedents to the contrary are quoted in the judgments in Cook *v.* Imperial Tobacco Co. Ltd. (1922).[3] In this case, however, the Court of Appeal decided that the *in forma pauperis* procedure of the High Court had always been purely statutory and could not therefore be extended to the County Court as if it were a "general principle of practice" but would require express exactment.

The Judges, in giving their decision, pointed out the injustice which might result and recommended further consideration of the whole question by the appropriate authority. This was no doubt partly responsible for the appointment of the Committee under the chairmanship of Mr. Justice Finlay, to which reference has been made above in connection with the criminal courts. The constitution of this Committee was criticized by both *The Law Journal* and the *Law Times*,[4] the latter saying,

> With one or two exceptions all the members seem singularly out of touch with the legal troubles of the poor. Fewer official members and the inclusion of a County Court Judge and a Stipendiary Magistrate, together with a representative of one of the numerous settlements, would have made for more efficiency in unravelling what is admittedly an exceedingly difficult subject.

The Committee's report on proceedings in the County Courts [5] was not ready until the beginning of 1928 and then the only legal aid which it recommended was in the small number of cases which are remitted from the High Court.[6] The Poor Persons' Rules were duly amended to cover this point and all other cases in the County Court remain dependent on the charitable, co-operative or speculative efforts of the organizations described in the Report.

The charitable organizations interested in the subject were not

[1] 1849 8 *C.B.*, 447; 19 *L.J.C.P.*, 42; 79 *R.R.*, 566.
[2] 47 *L.J.*, 48.
[3] 2 *K.B.*, 158; 91 *L.J.K.B.*, 771.
[4] 60 *L.J.*, 361; 159 *L.T.*, 317.
[5] Cmd. 3016.
[6] Para. 15.

impressed by the Committee's findings that better facilities for litigation were not necessary and a conference was called by the Legal Aid Committee of the London Council of Social Service [1] as a result of which, in 1929, the Bentham Committee was founded, with the object of improving and co-ordinating the activities of Poor Man's Lawyers in London. The Bentham Committee has an office at No. 1, Lincoln's Inn Fields, with a paid Almoner and Secretary, and, while not subject in any way to the Law Society or the Bar Council, it has a distinguished list of lawyers associated with it and its Regulations have been well described as "markedly influenced by professional ethics or etiquette".

It set out to improve the standard of free legal advice and also to provide assistance with litigation in the County Courts and Police Courts of the administrative County of London. A Cases Fund was built up to assist poor litigants with fees and disbursements, and rotas of solicitors and barristers who were willing to conduct these cases were formed. No charge is made to the poor person in any event and, if costs are awarded against his opponent they are donated to the Committee. Six times as many cases were referred to the Committee in 1938 as in 1929.

The Committee always had difficulty in securing sufficient solicitors to conduct cases and the two largest affiiliated centres, Cambridge House and Toynbee Hall made their own arrangements for providing court action where necessary, while some of the other centres found the Committee's procedure too slow and troublesome and referred cases to their friends. At Toynbee Hall a solicitor was paid a yearly retaining fee and disbursements to take up cases which required action in the County Court or, very occasionally, in the Police Court. The solicitor was entitled to retain any costs which might be awarded against the opponent; 52 cases were referred to solicitors in 1938.

At Cambridge House the system before 1939 was similar to that adopted by most of the provincial Poor Man's Lawyer Associations that had grown up. That is to say no inducement was offered to the solicitors who conducted cases other than a guarantee for disbursements and the prospect of recovering costs from the opponent, if successful. As at Manchester, but not Liverpool, the solicitors were entitled to charge in a proper case but was expected to take his client's circumstances into account; at Birmingham the solicitors are not allowed to charge their own

[1] 165 *L.T.*, 402; 72 *S.J.*, 306.

clients. At Hull the conducting solicitors retain two-thirds of the costs recovered from the opposing party, one-third being paid into the funds of the association.

In addition to these purely philanthropic developments much is done to assist workmen by Trade Unions and, to a lesser extent, by Approved Societies. The Unions, of course, will only act for their own members and usually only in cases of accident at work or employment troubles; some of them do not provide legal services at all. A few of the Approved Societies give legal assistance to members in accident cases with a view to reducing their liability under the National Health Insurance Acts. Apart from these and a few other miscellaneous organizations there is a considerable amount of litigation which is divided between those few charitable Poor Man's Lawyers which give this assistance and speculative solicitors or spurious Legal Aid Societies. Particulars of the developments which have taken place during the war are given in the next chapter.

CHAPTER V

LEGAL ADVICE

While legal aid in the courts has always been regarded as being to some extent the responsibility of the State, legal advice has, until recent years, received no official recognition.

Injustice arises more obviously from inability to contest a case in court but it requires little thought to realize that the poor are also severely handicapped when they wish to ascertain their legal position and to obtain assistance short of court proceedings. The poor are less educated and informed ; they have not, like the more wealthy man, a lawyer friend whom they can casually ask for explanation of a trifling point, and often they cannot afford to pay a solicitor's fee for mere advice much less the larger fees in which they may become involved if the work to be done proves to be substantial. As Dr. E. J. Cohn has written,[1] " In our society it has become expensive not only to litigate but even to avoid litigation, and to keep on the straight (and often narrow) road of lawfulness." Yet the poor, like other citizens, are presumed to know the law, and have to bear the brunt of their ignorance even if they have no way of remedying it.

It was not theory, however, which gave rise to " Poor Man's Lawyer Centres " in the slums of London and provincial cities, it was the first-hand experience of social workers at Social Service Settlements, who found themselves being asked for help on legal, as on other, questions. If there were no lawyers connected with the Settlement, someone usually had a lawyer friend who could help. Often the lawyer would find it necessary to see the enquirer before he could give his answer and would come down to the Settlement one evening. Perhaps there would be a few other enquiries which he might as well deal with at the same time. When this had happened once or twice it became obvious that there was a demand for a regular weekly sitting, and lawyers who had once experienced the pleasure of seeing a harassed workman or a tearful wife leave the room, grateful and relieved, after a few words of explanation and advice, were only too willing to offer this small service.

How else, indeed, could these people learn whether the law provided any remedy for their case and whether there was an

[1] 59 *L.Q.R.* (July 1943), 252.

alternative to retaking their goods by force or trying to get their rights by threats? There has always been a Common Law right to go to a magistrate for advice but often magistrates were not lawyers; nor were the conditions of the court room conducive to the discussion of the intimate details of one's life. Court Missionaries and organizations such as the Women's and Children's Protection Society could help with certain types of personal problems, local authorities had many powers in connection with housing, newspapers answered legal questions in their columns, but the vast problem of giving qualified professional advice on legal problems as a whole was tackled only by the Poor Man's Lawyers.

It was in the 1890's, a decade usually associated with activities of a very different nature, that these worthy enterprises first came into being. Mansfield House in Canning Town was probably the first of all *; it was soon followed by Toynbee Hall and Cambridge House. Manchester provided the earliest provincial Poor Man's Lawyer about fifty years ago.

As time went on the work grew and grew. Several lawyers would come down together; rotas were formed; at some centres clerical help was obtained and records kept for use at subsequent interviews; a few reference books were provided. At each centre the rules and methods varied, so that it might be said that the only thing they had in common was the central idea of providing legal advice free to poor people through the charitable efforts of solicitors and barristers.

When in 1913 some alteration of the 1883 Rules relating to High Court procedure obviously had to be made, the Law Society called a conference of Poor Man's Lawyers, believing that in an extension of their work a solution of the difficulty might be reached by disposing of many of the cases before litigation was commenced. A Constitution and Regulations for the "Poor Man's Lawyer Association of London" were approved but the Association was never formed and instead of official support for legal advice work the new measures which were adopted related only to litigation.[1] Further ineffective attempts were made to call attention to the need for legal advice when the Poor Persons' Rules broke down in 1922 and 1923,[2] and when the Committee

* 1890. A Legal Aid Centre modelled on the Mansfield House P.M.L. was started in Jersey City, U.S.A., in 1894. Cambridge House P.M.L. provided the model for the Belfast Legal Dispensary.

[1] Annual Reports 1913 and 1914; 48 *L.J.*, 180 and 288; 57 *S.J.*, 383.

[2] 156 *L.T.*, 333 and 350; 87 *J.P.*, 86; 60 *L.J.*, 136.

under Mr. Justice Finlay reported in 1928 on the question of legal aid in the County Courts, stress was laid on the valuable work done by Poor Man's Lawyers and the desirability of extending them, but this extension was still left to voluntary efforts.[1]

Co-operation was never the strong point of Poor Man's Lawyer organizations, each centre preferring to maintain its own methods and independence, but in the large towns amalgamation was eventually effected and Poor Man's Lawyer Associations formed. This led to a reduction in the variety of systems existing side by side in a particular district, to a more impressive appeal for funds, more economical expenditure and better organization in general. Some sort of central office becomes necessary when there is a large number of lawyers co-operating in a scheme and this again improves the standard of the centres through the supervision which it is able to exercise, and leads towards a development of the scope of the work.

The Manchester and Salford Poor Man's Lawyer Association for some time shared the office of the local Poor Persons' Committee but now has a separate office with a full-time salaried assistant secretary. Cases requiring representation are allotted to conducting solicitors through this office and any solicitor on the rota who declines to accept a case has to report the reasons for his refusal to the assistant secretary. Solicitors must also, on request, report the result of any cases taken up by them. All this helps to raise the standard of the work done. The Liverpool Association is more closely connected with general social service and the head office of the Personal Service Society acts as the central office for the Poor Man's Lawyers. In Birmingham the Law Society's premises and staff are used.

In 1938–9 the Manchester and Salford Poor Man's Lawyer Association dealt with 3,965 cases and Birmingham, 4,328. There were about 70 Poor Man's Lawyer centres in the provinces, though many of them were very small, and 55 (non-political) centres in London, this number having been increased from the 27 that existed in 1928 largely by the efforts of the Bentham Committee. Further particulars of the working of some of the schemes will be found in Appendix A.

The war had an immediate and devastating effect on the valuable work being done by Poor Man's Lawyers. The organization, such as it was, depended on the willingness of lawyers to sacrifice their spare time. The younger men were

[1] Cmd. 3016, paras. 5–10 and 20.

called up and the older members of the profession had their hands full with their own work and war-time activities. A great many centres closed down ; instead of 55 centres the Bentham Committee listed 41, of which 17 were temporarily closed * ; the black out and war-time difficulties made others inaccessible to many people ; practically everywhere the number of cases dealt with dropped considerably.

At the same time the demand for legal advice increased. Many new Acts and Regulations affecting the poorer people were passed ; bombing and the increase of road accidents, bad housing conditions and the inevitable wave of domestic troubles made it more necessary than ever, if only in the interests of morale, that legal advice for the poor should be available.

The one bright spot in the picture was the setting up of Citizens' Advice Bureaux. These Bureaux, organized by the social service societies, were already planned in readiness for the demand for general information and advice which the war would bring. They were not equipped to deal with legal problems but the need for some method of dealing with such problems was recognized and became more and more obvious as time went on.

It was to meet this need that one of the most interesting developments in the history of the Poor Man's Lawyer was embarked upon—the opening of a Free Legal Advice Centre, open at ordinary office hours, as well as one evening a week, for the use of local people and all the Citizens' Advice Bureaux in South London and even farther afield.

At first the organization consisted of a full time Honorary Secretary with assistance for typing and filing, and the advising was done by solicitors and barristers on a rota. Gradually the rota dwindled as lawyers were called to other forms of service and in any event the system did not prove very satisfactory. Some of the lawyers who had generously offered their services might be expert on criminal law or divorce but would insist on advising on the Rent Restriction Acts, about which they knew nothing. After advising on hundreds of matrimonial cases one solicitor was found to be unaware that a divorce could not normally be obtained within three years of the marriage.

The bulk of the work came to be done by two volunteers who gave all or practically all their time to it, with occasional help from solicitors in private practice. The gaps in their knowledge were filled out and much of their time saved by a system of " corre-

* In 1944 there were 40, of which 14 were temporarily closed.

sponding advisers" who wrote out opinions on specialized or complicated problems. Of necessity a great deal of negotiation and correspondence had to be undertaken at the centre because there were few solicitors willing to undertake unremunerative cases. As a result of a most generous offer by one solicitor, however, a small number of the more important and difficult cases were negotiated or fought by his firm in a thorough and able manner, the Cases Fund of the centre providing disbursements, when necessary, and any costs recovered from the opposing party being donated to the Fund. A few other solicitors occasionally took cases on the same basis.

Later it became impossible to get the same amount of unpaid help and small payments had to be made for clerical help and to the advisers and the conducting solicitor. These were very small however and the necessary funds were provided by the Pilgrim Trust, the Ministry of Health grant made to the centre for its Citizens' Advice Bureau work, and donations, including considerable sums from the applicants themselves.

The scale of the work done may be gathered from the following figures (compared with about 3,000 interviews per annum before the war):

	New Cases	Interviews	Letters	Telephone consultations
1941 .	4,218	6,212	2,350	(included in interviews)
1942 .	4,698	7,399	4,056	"
1943 .	4,367	6,714	4,560	678

The following approximate figures give a rough indication of the amount of money obtained or saved for applicants in the cases handled in 1942:

	£	s.	d.
Lump sums saved or recovered	1,836	6	6
Annual value of weekly sums saved or recovered . .	795	7	8
Sums recovered by solicitors acting free of charge on behalf of the centre:			
By negotiations.	2,888	0	0
By proceedings	542	10	0
	£6,062	4	2

The arrangements first made for London Citizens' Advice Bureaux north of the Thames did not prove satisfactory and when they finally came to an end a Legal Advice Centre was opened at the Mary Ward Settlement. This was operated very much on the lines of Cambridge House, the Centre which has just been described, but preserving its own independence. It was soon handling nearly as many cases as the centre in South London.

In the provinces also the advent of the Citizens' Advice Bureaux made itself felt. Although many of the old Poor Man's Lawyer schemes collapsed with the outbreak of war there is more legal advice provided now than at any time before, but it is quite clear that a very high proportion of the advice is given by social workers and not by lawyers, as will be seen from the reports on Bristol and Reading in Appendix A.

Only a few Citizens' Advice Bureaux are unable to provide any legal advice at all but equally few have anything approaching adequate facilities. The most rudimentary system in use is for the Citizens' Advice Bureau to consult a friendly solicitor over the telephone and then to convey the advice to the applicant ; in some places an appointment can be made to see the solicitor at his office, and there are a few fortunate bureaux where a solicitor attends regularly every week to deal with the applicants who have been told to call.

But whatever the system the mere existence of Citizens' Advice Bureaux is in itself a great help. Whereas before the war a person with a legal problem might be unaware of any way of getting advice unless he happened to have seen a notice advertising a Poor Man's Lawyer or to have been informed of the existence of one by neighbours, he now can go to the Citizens' Advice Bureau or Central Information Bureau, and either have his query dealt with there or be referred to the appropriate organization. Moreover, a large body of social workers has come into being, anxious to assist the poor with their difficulties and aware of the importance of legal aid.

The growing consciousness of the need for better facilities led the National Council of Social Service to approach the Law Society early in the war and to work out with them a scheme for legal assistance in connection with Citizens' Advice Bureaux in the provinces. This scheme is important because it introduces the revolutionary principle of payment of reduced fees. One of the most exasperating features of free legal aid work is that, although finance is a constant source of difficulty, the scheme cannot be made wholly or partially self-supporting by charging reduced fees because of the professional fear of undercutting, and while there are many people who can afford to pay a proportion of the usual fees for professional services, and who are anxious to do so, no charge whatever can be made by the organization or, strictly speaking, by the solicitor to whom a case is referred by the organization, although the latter is frequently done in practice.

The Citizens' Advice Bureau scheme, which was approved by the Law Society in 1940, was as follows:

Each provincial Law Society should provide one or more legal advice centres to serve the Citizens' Advice Bureaux within its area. At each centre there should be a clerk to interview the applicants, take particulars of his means and the nature of his case and collect any fee which might be due.

A rota should be prepared by the Law Society of solicitors and barristers willing to attend and advise at the centre. Assistance beyond mere advice should be given through a second list, under the charge of a rota manager, of solicitors willing to conduct cases on the terms of the scheme. Cases should be allotted in such a way that the burden and profit would be evenly distributed. A solicitor on the list should only be entitled to refuse a case allotted to him if he was instructed by another interested party or the matter was of a class that he did not undertake or on some other special ground, and a written report must be sent to the rota manager on the completion of the case. If he wished, the applicant might choose a solicitor he had previously instructed.

The charge for the services varied according to the means of the applicant, who were divided into three categories:

A.—If the income of the applicant's household, after deduction of rent did not exceed—

In the case of a single person, £2.

In the case of a married person, £2 10*s.*, plus 7*s.* 6*d.* for each child, and, if the readily realizable capital assets of the applicant (excluding clothes, the tools of his trade and the subject-matter of the application) did not exceed £50, all services free except for disbursements.

B.—If the corresponding figures are £3 10*s.* (single), £4 (married) plus 7*s.* 6*d.* for each child and £100 (capital), advice should be given for 3*s.* an interview and further assistance at one-third of the usual charges, plus full disbursements.

C.—If the corresponding figures are £5 (single), £5 10*s.* (married) plus 7*s.* 6*d.* for each child, and £150 (capital), advice should be given for 6*s.* per interview and further assistance at two-thirds of the usual profit charges plus full disbursements.

The solicitors should be entitled to retain any costs recovered from third parties. Fees for advice should be divided amongst the advisers in proportion to their share in the work.

The scheme was more remarkable for the principles which it introduced than for its practical effect, but having regard to the wartime shortage of solicitors this was not surprising; those Law Societies which were most likely to accept the scheme already had a Poor Man's Lawyer functioning and did not see the necessity for change during the emergency, and most of the other Societies felt unable to undertake further work under existing circumstances.

Seventeen out of nearly one hundred Law Societies agreed to operate the scheme, but in several cases it never came into operation; in practically all districts the numbers dealt with are amazingly small, and in some the scheme appears to have been allowed to lapse and to have become confused with the provision of legal aid to the Forces which will be described later. All the Law Societies which operated the scheme made modifications in the original proposals; Harrogate, for instance, applied it only to advice and Wolverhampton considerably cut down the scale of means. In spite of these somewhat disappointing results the fact that the scheme was proposed by the Law Society at all and was accepted in some of the provincial towns and cities is a great step forward and is an indication of the future direction of legal aid when conditions are more favourable after the war.

Leaving the effects of the formation of Citizens' Advice Bureaux we come to the other prominent force in war-time developments in this field—the requirements of the Armed Forces. As in the case of divorce, legal advice was deemed necessary "in order to meet the difficulties experienced by soldiers and members of the A.T.S. in obtaining, under war conditions, advice and assistance in their civil legal problems".

A.C.I. 1398 of 4th July, 1942, lays down the scheme, which applies to members of the Army and A.T.S. up to and including the rank of sergeants, provided that they have not sufficient private resources to employ their own legal advisers. The scheme covers only advice; if more than drafting a letter is required the adviser is to endeavour to put the soldier in touch with a solicitor. Advisers consist of serving or civilian volunteers, they are not always lawyers but at some stations consist of the chaplain or some other officer.

In addition, each Command has a Command Legal Aid (Civil Affairs) Section staffed by two officers, with four ranks as clerks, or in the case of the London Section four officers and eight clerks. The functions of the sections are to supervise the Legal Advice Bureaux and to assist the Law Societies and solicitors co-operating in the scheme. Although they are by no means limited to that function the bureaux and legal aid sections are useful links with the Services Divorce Department. Following the example of the War Office the Air Ministry joined in the scheme in November 1942 and Legal Aid Sections have now been established in some districts for men in the Royal Navy.

Originally the London and Scottish Sections dealt with troops overseas, but it was soon found desirable that the work should be done on the spot as far as possible and there are now Advice Bureaux for nearly all Commands overseas and Legal Aid Sections for the larger Commands. The number of cases has proved much larger than was anticipated and it continually increases. The Sections alone (not the Advice Bureaux) had dealt with over 30,000 cases by the end of 1943 and representations have been made to the military authorities that an immediate increase in the staffs of the Sections is necessary to prevent a breakdown of the Services Divorce scheme which is run in co-operation with the Legal Aid Scheme.[1]

Sufficient has been said to show that legal advice is not an unimportant part of legal aid, or, indeed, of the administration of justice. If the War Office, Air Ministry and Admiralty find it necessary, in the midst of a war, to set up schemes of this sort, if the large Settlements have maintained Poor Man's Lawyers over a period of 50 years and the social service organizations and Law Societies in various parts of the country have sponsored this work; if, above all, a Departmental Committee has reported that any difficulties which the poor may have with regard to the administration of justice can be solved by the provision of legal advice, it behoves us to consider carefully whether the present provision of advice is satisfactory in quality and quantity and, if it is not, how that state of affairs can be remedied without delay. These matters are dealt with in the second part of this book.

[1] Law Society's Annual Report, 1944.

CHAPTER VI

LEGAL AID IN OTHER COUNTRIES

A comparative study of legal aid is not easy without a knowledge of the general system of law and procedure in force in the countries under consideration and some people are apt to maintain, especially when the practice in other countries is quoted in support of a point of view with which they do not agree, that we are quite capable of managing our own affairs and that our arrangements cannot be compared with those of countries where entirely different conditions obtain. The constructive results which can be achieved by the comparative approach have, however, been recently demonstrated by the stimulating article by Dr. E. J. Cohn in the *Law Quarterly Review*,[1] and some of the statements of Departmental Committees and others with regard to legal aid could never have been made if they had had knowledge of the experience of other countries.

The following study starts with the British Empire, and it will be seen that in most of these countries the English provisions have been adopted after a considerable time-lag; in Australia, however, some of the States have begun to take a line of their own. This tendency to adopt the system of the country with which one has the closest affinity is fairly common and some European examples are given subsequently.

Scotland.—Scotland had statutory provision for legal aid even earlier than England. For its language alone the Statute deserves quotation:

Parliament at Perth March 12th, 1424

Cap 24 (1424 cap. 45) Anent billis of complayntis. . . . Gif there be onie pure creature, for faulte of cunning or expenses, that cannot, nor may not follow his cause, the King, for the love of God, sall ordaine the judge before quhom the cause suld be determined, to purwey and get a leill and wise advocate to follow sik pure creatures causes; and gif sik causes be obtained the wranger sal assyith baith the partie skaithed and the advocate's coastes and travel.

In order to understand the modern provisions it should be explained that the civil courts in Scotland consist of the Sheriff Courts, which are district courts, in many ways analogous to

[1] 59 *L.Q.R.*, 250–71, 359–77.

our County Courts but also with jurisdiction in separation and affiliation cases, and the Court of Session. The Court of Session is the Supreme Court in Scotland and is the Court of Appeal as well as court of first instance in some matters. Most poor persons' cases are dealt with in the Sheriff Courts ; such cases as come before the Court of Session are mostly divorce cases.

Representation in civil and criminal cases is provided by the *Agents of the Poor.* In the Court of Session, six advocates, and at least four Writers to the Signet and four solicitors, are appointed annually by their respective professional organizations. At the same time two Advocates, a Writer to the Signet and a Solicitor are appointed to act as Reporters on *Probabilis Causa* and to investigate the means of applicants. It is usual for the most recent members of the professions to be appointed for these duties.

A person applying for " the benefit of the Poor's Roll " must lodge an Affidavit as to his means with the clerk in charge of the Poor's Roll. A solicitor is allotted to him who submits a memorandum on the case to the Reporters on *Probabilis Causa* and to the opposing party to the proposed suit, who is given an opportunity of appearing before the Reporters before they report to the Court. If the Court receives a favourable report on means and, in a civil case, on *probabilis causa,* the Poor Person is referred to a Writer to the Signet or a solicitor, and an advocate is allotted to him. He is not required to make any payment into Court and he is provisionally exempt from all court fees and lawyers' fees but must pay out-of-pocket expenses. The lawyers receive no fees unless costs are recovered from the opposing party.

In the Sheriff Courts the procedure is much the same except that the number of Agents varies for each Court (6 for Edinburgh, 4 for Dundee, 26 for Glasgow), and the certificate of poverty is granted by the Public Assistance Officer. A high proportion of the cases in these courts concern affiliation and separation.

In all the courts the opponent of the poor person has the same rights and liabilities as to costs as in an ordinary case. There is no fixed standard as to the amount of means which constitutes a poor person, but an income limit of £2 or 35*s.* a week appears to be usual, although in some districts more would be allowed where there were several children. There is no appeal against a refusal of the benefit of the Poor's Roll.

The Agents of the Poor are not obliged to act in Police Court Cases, but in Dundee the four agents are prepared to do so and share between them the sum of £50 granted by the Town Council for the defence of accused poor persons. A grant of £30 is similarly made by the Edinburgh Town Council. It has been officially recommended that large towns should be under an obligation to provide this aid.

This system of the annual election of members of the profession to undertake voluntary duties in connection with the poor is found in other countries. In most cases, however, it is either obligatory or customary to appoint men of some years' standing in the profession ; the appointment of the most recent recruits can hardly be regarded as desirable. But the chief complaint about the system comes from the Poor's Agents, who have long maintained that it casts too heavy a burden upon them. In Glasgow a practice has grown up which, if not illegal, is contrary to the spirit of the rules, of demanding payment of £10 or £20 from the poor person,[1] and the Paisley Faculty of Procurators has tried to alleviate the position of the Agents by inviting its members to subscribe to a fund out of which the two junior Agents of the Poor are paid £20 each every year.[2]

These facts were brought out in 1937 in the Report of a Committee appointed by the Secretary of State for Scotland, which confirmed that the system might break down if radical changes were not soon made.[3] Some of the alterations which were recommended for the Sheriff Courts were that admission to the Poor's Roll should be granted by the Reporters appointed by the professional bodies, but with a right of appeal to the Sheriff Substitute.[4] The Reporters in each district should have a Solicitor as full-time or part-time salaried Clerk, with the necessary staff, who would investigate cases, give legal advice and grant applications in clear cases. Applicants should pay something, however small, both for advice and litigation, the amount being fixed by the Reporters. Agents should only receive fees if successful but should be entitled to repayment of all outlays incurred by them. The salaries and administration expenses involved in these proposals (which have not yet been adopted) and certain outlays should be paid by the Treasury.[5] It was also recommended that it should be the duty of the Local Authority in large towns to provide out of local funds a

[1] Report of the Poor Persons' Representation (Scotland) Committee, Cmd. 5435 para. 16.

[2] Cmd. 5435, para. 28. [3] Cmd. 5435, para. 2.

[4] Cmd. 5435, paras. 41 and 42. [5] Cmd. 5435, paras. 40–50.

Public Defensor for poor persons accused before the Police Courts.[1]

In addition to representation in all courts (with the exception of some Police Courts) Scotland boasts a well-established Legal Advice Centre in its capital. This is the Edinburgh Legal Dispensary, formed in 1900, and managed by a Board of Directors appointed by each of the four legal professional bodies. It is open one night a week and normally advice is only given to applicants whose income does not exceed £3 a week. Records are kept, correspondence is undertaken and every effort is made to settle cases without proceedings, litigation being left entirely to the Agents of the Poor. The following figures for consultations show its development:

1900–1	274	1925–6	2,434
1905–6	1,232	1930–1	3,243
1910–11	2,032	1935–6	3,161
1915–16	1,513	1938–9	3,471
1920–1	1,672		

Thirty lawyers were taking part in the scheme before the war. Four lawyers attended each night and between them saw an average of over 69 people a night, so that frequently cases had to be taken away for further consideration.

As in other organizations of the same sort the work suffered greatly during the war. There are now only seventeen lawyers available, of whom three attend each night. The figures for the last four years were 2,655, 2,441, 2,030, 2,076.

In Glasgow there are centres at the Pierce Institute, Govan, and at the University Settlement, under the Glasgow University Law Society, where students who have recently qualified and who are in their final year give advice, and there are two centres under the Glasgow Society of Social Service. Numbers are small in each case.

Northern Ireland.—In *Northern Ireland* the system which obtained in England before 1914 is still in force, including the requirements that the applicant must not be worth more than £25 and must produce a Counsel's Opinion.

But, although in 1925 the Northern Ireland Law Society adopted a resolution stating strongly that no alteration was necessary or desirable,[2] it had changed its opinion by 1939 and

[1] Cmd. 5435, para. 59.

[2] League of Nations, *Legal Aid for the Poor* (v. Legal 1927, v. 27). This report contains information as to the facilities in a large number of countries up to 1924 or 1925.

had asked for a scheme to be formulated similar to that of the English Poor Persons' Procedure. Such a scheme has been adopted and it is expected that it will shortly come into force.

The change in attitude was probably due to the experience gained by the Advice Centre in Belfast set up by the Bar Council, Law Society and Belfast Council of Social Welfare in January 1937. After less than two years' working the provision of advice was supplemented by representation in the Police and County Courts through panels of volunteers. As at Cambridge House, costs recovered by solicitors, less disbursements, are devoted to a Cases Fund, which provides assistance for needy applicants. The figures for advice for the years 1937 to 1943 are as follows:

66, 99, 95, 238, 360, 760, 436

A proposal to start a Centre in Londonderry was frustrated by the War.

Eire.—In *Eire* the old English *in forma pauperis* procedure is in force in the High Court and there are no provisions for the Circuit Court and District Court, except power to remit Court fees in the latter. The efforts of Trade Unions and voluntary Societies to fill these gaps are admitted to be inadequate.

There is no legal aid in criminal cases except on capital charges.

Canada.—In some provinces there are no provisions, in others court fees can be remitted and occasionally representation is provided. Some local bars have made voluntary efforts to help poor litigants and sometimes soldiers overseas can sue for divorce for about half the usual cost.

India.—British India has no official provision for legal aid. But there is a Bombay Legal Aid Society and there may be others.

New Zealand.—At present there is only the usual *in forma pauperis* procedure. In 1939 *The Poor Persons' Legal Aid Act* was passed but the Regulations necessary to bring it into operation have not yet been enacted owing to the war and the shortage of solicitors.

The draft Regulations are on the lines of the English system but " all practitioners would automatically be on the lists of those available to conduct the cases ", which is presumably a gentle way of saying that all solicitors and counsel would be under compulsion to act.

South Africa.—In the Superior Courts of South Africa there is an *in forma pauperis* procedure limited to applicants who are not worth more than £25, or in some States, £10. Court fees are reduced and an advocate is provided.

In civil cases in the inferior (magistrates') courts a person who cannot pay the court fees and charges is exempted therefrom except for certain out-of-pocket expenses. An attorney can be appointed if the applicant is illiterate, or for some other reason unable to conduct his case in person.

In addition there is a Legal Aid Bureau in Johannesburg inaugurated in 1935 or 1937 by the Johannesburg Society of Advocates and the Incorporated Law Society of the Transvaal.[1] A retired magistrate, assisted by a retired Court Interpreter, was originally in charge of the Bureau which provided—

1. Legal advice of an elementary nature in non-criminal matters and assistance as regards official procedure.
2. Professional representation of indigent accused persons.

The advocates and attorneys on the panels are paid reduced fees by the Bureau, which derives its funds partly from the Institute of Race Relations and partly from private donations. Sometimes the accused or his friends pay the reduced fees.

In 1939 the Bureau began to undertake civil business, including non-litigious work. In 1943 the staff consisted of two full-time women attorneys, with clerks and interpreters. They were dealing with 3,000 cases per annum, involving 7,200 interviews and maintained that the work could never be done adequately until Goverment funds were made available.

Australia.—The position is more encouraging in Australia. In 1925, when a Report was made to the League of Nations, the English *in forma pauperis* rules were in force in the Supreme Court, but in some of the States there were improvements on these rules and many developments have taken place in recent years.

In *Queensland*,[2] for instance, the Public Curator may be required by the Minister of Justice to render to any Poor Person or accused person, legal aid in any legal proceedings and may instruct the office, or an outside solicitor or counsel and fix the fees payable. Legal advice is given by the Department of Justice.

In *South Australia* the £25 limit was increased in 1925 to £100 and the Judge was given power to order the Sheriff to pay out of State funds—

[1] Department of Justice Annual Report, 1938. The more recent information was kindly supplied to me by a correspondent from *Libertas*, April 1943, (Vol. 3, No. 5).
[2] *Public Curator Act*, 1915.

(*a*) the fees and expenses of the Poor Persons' witnesses ;
(*b*) the expenses of taking evidence on commission.

The Governor was also given the power to appoint a public solicitor to take all Poor Persons' cases.

In 1936 a further Act [1] gave the Attorney-General power to remit or reduce, conditionally or otherwise, any fees payable to the State and he may order any necessary copies of documents to be supplied free or at a reduced charge.

In *New South Wales*, the means test was £50, instead of £25, and household furniture was not taken into account. There was also a Legal Aid Office under the control of a barrister, with a staff consisting of a solicitor and clerical officers of the public service. The procedure has been greatly extended by the *Legal Assistance Act*, 1943. This gives the Government power to appoint a Public Solicitor and any necessary staff. Applications are made to, and granted by, the Public Solicitor, who may ask any barrister or solicitor who has volunteered his services, for a report or opinion.

The provisions apply to any person—

(i) who does not own property worth more than £100 excluding, in addition to the usual items, household furniture used by the applicant in his home and a dwelling house owned and used by the applicant as his home, where the value of his interest does not exceed £750, and

(ii) whose income, after deducting £50 for each dependant, does not exceed the " needs basic wage " by more than a certain amount.

Representation is provided by the Public Solicitor, a member of his staff, or by a solicitor, and possibly a barrister, on his panel. It seems that the lawyers on the panel receive no fees if unsuccessful.

Amongst other benefits the Public Solicitor may in a case of hardship provide the Poor Persons' necessary disbursements out of a fund maintained for the purpose.

In *Victoria* [2] also there is a Public Solicitor appointed to act in Poor Persons' Cases. The capital test is £50. Any costs which the Poor Person would normally receive are paid to revenue.

In *Tasmania* [3] the legal aid certificate is granted by a Committee of the Law Society. The financial limits are roughly the

[1] *Poor Persons' Legal Assistance Act*, 1936.
[2] *Poor Persons' Legal Assistance Act*, 1928.
[3] *Supreme Court Civil Procedure Act*, 1932, O. xviii.

same as in England, but from the computation of the applicant's capital are excluded household furniture and equipment used in his home up to the value of £40.

In *Western Australia* there was a *Poor Persons' Legal Assistance Act* in 1928 which was amended in 1931. To qualify for a grant an applicant must be—

(i) not worth more than £50 (with the usual items excluded), and not have earned the basic wage declared under the Industrial Arbitration Acts 1912–25 during the previous twelve months, or

(ii) any person " who proves that special circumstances incidental to his case necessitate legal attention which his means do not enable him to obtain ".

The provisions apply to the Local Courts as well as the Supreme Court.

Applications are made, through the Attorney-General, to a committee of the Law Society, which allots a practitioner.

If the Poor Person is awarded costs, they are paid to the Crown ; also, if the Poor Person recovers more than £50, up to one-quarter of the amount recovered may be taken by the Crown.

In addition to the usual benefits, the expenses of witnesses, who have been certified as necessary for the proceedings, are provided. Originally costs for which the Poor Person was made liable were paid by the Crown but this was rescinded in 1931.

The practitioners are paid by the Crown their out-of-pocket expenses and the following fees :

	£	s.	d.
For defending a prisoner on a capital charge	8	8	0
For defending an aboriginal native charged with murder .	3	3	0

Two-thirds of these sums for other indictable offences.

In civil cases the fees are 25 per cent. of the usual Local Court scale costs or 10 per cent. of the usual Supreme Court or Appeal Court scale costs. On the recommendation of the Court the Attorney-General may increase the fees.

Turning now to the Continent an example of the type of legislation found in most European countries is provided by the Austrian Code of Civil Procedure, 1895. Very similar provisions apply to Germany, Czechslovakia, Danzig, and many Swiss cantons ; they may be summarized as follows :

Austria.—§ 63. Any person who is not in a position to pay the costs of an action without encroaching upon the resources necessary for the maintenance of himself and his family may be granted free legal aid.

§ 64. The grant confers :

1. The right to request a free advocate where an advocate is necessary by law or where the trial is in a court in a locality outside the applicant's normal domicile or residence.

2. Exemption from giving security for costs.

3. Provisional exemption from stamp duties and other Treasury dues arising out of the action, fees of officers of the court and bailiffs, fees for execution of judgments and those due to witnesses and experts, the cost of copying records and annexed documents and of abstracts made by the court, the cost of his representatives or advocates. These costs and expenses shall be provisionally defrayed by the Treasury.

§ 65. Applications must be made in writing or verbally to the competent court of first instance, accompanied by a certificate which must mention his income and the names of his dependants and explicitly state his inability to pay the costs. The certificate shall be issued by the mayor of the applicant's commune and endorsed by the chief administrative authority.

§ 66. The actual appointment of the advocate shall be made by the competent committee of the Chamber of Advocates.

All the fees and expenses mentioned in § 64 are payable by the opposing party if condemned to pay costs.

There are penal provisions relating to the making of false declarations and the issue of false certificates.

There is another group of States where the procedure on application is more elaborate, so that the application takes on the form of a preliminary trial of the case with a view to a possible conciliation. In Belgium, France, Italy, Monaco and also in Haiti there is a special bureau or commission attached to each court for the purpose of these applications. Belgium may be taken as an example.

Belgium.—Legal Aid in Belgium was first provided by a decree of 14th December, 1810, amended by the Law of 30th July, 1889, and subsequently by the Law of 29th June, 1929.

Aid is granted in all courts, even before administrative tribunals, and in all matters which require an advocate, notary or bailiff.

Persons who have some resources, but insufficient to pay the whole cost, can get aid on paying an amount which is fixed when the application is granted.

There are bureaux attached to each court and some of them are divided into several sections. Each section or bureau consists of a Judge, appointed by the court at the beginning of each year, assisted by the King's Procurator and with the Clerk of the Court acting as clerk to the bureau. An appeal against the bureau's decision can only be made by the Procurator General attached to the Court of Appeal.

The application is made verbally or in writing to the competent bureau. A day is fixed for the hearing and a copy of the Statement accompanying the application is sent to the opposing party, who is invited to attend. The parties may attend personally or may be represented by an advocate or by a representative approved by the bureau. The bureau hears the parties and endeavours to reconcile them. If settlement is reached the agreement is drawn up, signed by the parties and filed, and a copy is delivered to each of them. If no settlement can be reached immediately the bureau can order an adjournment for further information to be obtained and may instruct the King's Procurator to make enquiries.

If aid is granted an attorney, notary or bailiff, according to the circumstances, is appointed from a list drawn up by the respective professional organizations each year.

No court fees are payable in respect of the application for legal aid and all court fees in respect of the trial of the suit are provisionally remitted.

An advance is made to the Poor Person by the Ministry of Justice of all travelling and subsistence allowances of experts and witnesses, the fees of experts, the expenses of witnesses, the cost of any necessary advertisements, all authorized disbursements, and one-quarter of the salaries of bailiffs. These sums are recovered from the opposing party if he is ordered to pay costs, or from the Poor Person if he is in a position to pay them within thirty years.

The lawyers receive their fees if costs are awarded against the opposing party.

In many countries although the provisions relating to legal aid are generous it is probable that the actual administration of the provisions reduces their usefulness. This is obviously not the case in Sweden where both the spirit which informs the provisions and the number of people who make use of them leave no doubt as to the importance which legal aid is regarded as having in the administration of justice. The history of the development of the Swedish system is of some interest.

Sweden.[1]—In 1872 the town of Gothenburg appointed a special lawyer to assist needy people free of charge, or at a reduced fee, both in and out of court. Stockholm did the same in 1884 and by 1916 practically all the larger towns had established branches of " the poor man's advocate ".

The advocate did not devote himself exclusively to this work but carried on his private practice and it was found that the municipal work was neglected. In 1912 the advocates dealt with 1,445 cases, in 467 of which there was litigation.

In 1913 the work was reorganized in Stockholm under a full time Director and rapidly increased. The authorities took the view that " it was most important that the State should inform poor persons of their rights and facilitate their access to the courts ".

In 1919 and 1920 the Law concerning Free Legal Proceedings and the Royal Decree concerning the Grant of Government Subsidies to Public Legal Aid Institutions came into force.

The latter provides for the setting up of bureaux by the local authorities. It is not compulsory and development was slower than had been hoped ; in 1924 there were five bureaux and in 1938 there were bureaux in six towns and one province.

The bureaux qualify for a Government subsidy on three conditions :

(*a*) The institution must be under the control of a committee consisting of a Chairman and a Deputy Chairman appointed by the provincial Governor and at least two members appointed by the commune or communes which have set up the bureau.

(*b*) The work must be carried out in accordance with certain model Regulations.

(*c*) Statistics must be furnished to the Central Statistical Office.

The subsidy consists of a grant up to 3,000 kr. to start a new bureau and one-half of the annual debit balance for salaries, and office and other expenses. The remainder is paid by the local authority.

In 1923 the Stockholm bureau had a staff of a full-time salaried Director, five salaried lawyers, and a clerical staff of

[1] *Social Work and Legislation in Sweden,* 1938, provides the more recent information given here.

fifteen, the other bureaux had each a full-time Director and a clerk. The lawyers visit outlying districts from time to time. Out of a population of 425,000 the Stockholm bureau received 24,326 visits and wrote 18,790 letters in 1923.

The bureaux advise and conduct notarial business for anyone of small means. The applicant's statement as to means is normally accepted but there is power to call for further evidence.

The bureaux also conduct litigation but the actual grant of legal aid is made by the court and a private attorney may apply for legal aid on behalf of a client and be paid for the conduct of the case by the State if the client does not wish to be represented through the bureau. According to Gurney Champion 90 per cent. prefer to be represented by the bureau. When a lawyer from the bureau appears in a case he receives a fee from the State but, being salaried, he accounts for it to the bureau ; the fee is fixed by the Court. There are public bureaux, which appear to be similar, in Finland, Germany, Norway, Poland, and some American States.

The only qualification for legal aid in proceedings is the applicant's statement, confirmed by a public authority or well-known person, that he is not in a position to pay for the conduct of the proceedings. There is no requirement that the applicant must be justified in bringing his case, except that by an amending Act of 14th June, 1929, free legal proceedings are not to be granted to a party when it must be considered of extremely little importance to him that his case should be tried.

In addition to representation and exemption from court fees the State pays witnesses' allowances and copying charges. The aided person pays no fees unless his financial position improves, whether as a result of the proceedings or otherwise, within five years. If costs are awarded against the opponent they are paid to the State.

In 1935 the Bureaux and free legal proceedings cost the State 0·5 million kroner, as compared with 54·2 for unemployment (including unemployment insurance), 38·3 for Public Health and care of the sick, 55·9 for Pension Insurance, 13 for Sickness Insurance, 1·7 for assistance to the blind, and a total State expenditure for social purposes of 180 million.

Russia.[1]—Many people will be interested to know what the position is with regard to legal aid in Russia, but the truth of the matter appears to be that the problem does not arise in an acute

[1] See Ralph Millner : *Soviet Justice.*

form in that country. Lawyers' fees are relatively low and in litigation a sum is paid in advance for the whole case. Law and procedure are kept as simple as possible and the public is instructed in the law. Lawyers are not so highly trained and a litigant may not only conduct his own case but, with the leave of the court, may be represented by a friend. For advice nobody pays any fee unless the advice involves prolonged study of documents or complicated research; then the maximum fee is about 10*s*. The social responsibilities of the legal profession are greatly stressed and it is not unusual for cases to be conducted free of charge even when to do so is not compulsory.

In 1939 Moscow lawyers advised in 160,000 cases and, in 40,000 of these made no charge; they conducted 60,000 cases, 5,500 free of charge.

A person accused of crime is entitled to free representation if he cannot afford the fees and at the end of the case the court enquires into the applicant's means and decides what fee, if any, shall be paid. There are also certain civil cases where lawyers are obliged to act without fee—where a wife is claiming maintenance, in affiliation proceedings, and where a workman is claiming for injuries at work.

U.S.A.—To present anything more than the briefest summary of the position in America is beyond the scope of this report.

The Federal Statutes provide that legal aid shall be given to anyone who is unable to pay the costs of the proceedings except when the proceedings are not taken in good faith or are frivolous or malicious. Application is made to the trial court, accompanied by a statement on oath with regard to means and cause of action.

The grant exempts the assisted person from prepayment of fees and costs, i.e. witnesses' expenses, etc., and from giving security for costs, and the court may request any attorney to represent the assisted person without charge. The usual liability of the parties for the costs of opposing parties is not affected by the grant.

In addition to the Federal provisions there are different laws for each of the States, many of them providing less comprehensive aid than the Federal Statutes. An interesting feature of the aid given in criminal cases is that some States have a *Public Defender*, an official paid by the State, as opposed to *assigned counsel*, or a *Private Defender* as the official is called when appointed by some organization other than the State.

The problem created by the vast area and population of

America and the numerous different jurisdictions has led to far more scientific study of the subject of legal aid than in this country, although progress in some directions must necessarily be slower.

It was the difficulties of the immigrant that gave rise to the early formation of a legal aid organization in New York in 1876. As in Sweden the Attorney in charge was at first part-time and continued a private practice but later was engaged full time. Similar organizations were started in other big cities and the movement grew, slowly at first, then, after the first World War, with ever-increasing speed. Some of the organizations were formed into a *National Alliance* in 1912 and this gave way in 1923 to the National Association of Legal Aid Organizations, whose activities have had a tremendous effect on legal aid in the U.S.A. and, indirectly, abroad. It started with twenty-three constituent organizations. It worked at the improvement and standardization of record systems, financial and general organization, the formation of standards and ideals, publicity, and the gathering and dissemination of information, the institution of new legal aid organizations, of Small Claim's Courts, Defenders, conciliation and arbitration machinery. It contacted, and co-operated with, other national bodies, with the Bar Associations, Law Schools, Industrial Boards and Commissions, Government Labour officials and Social Welfare Organizations and it instituted the enquiry which resulted in the League of Nations Report, *Legal Aid for the Poor*, published in 1927.

The Bar Associations also played a large part in extending the availability of legal Services, under the guidance and encouragement of the American Bar Association, which in 1921 appointed a Standing Committee on Legal Aid and recommended other Bar Associations to do the same.

In 1941 there were 143 legal aid organizations in the U.S.A.,[1] of which some were run by Bar Associations, Law Schools, or charitable organizations, others were independent organizations and others municipal bureaux, and it is claimed that during the year they collected or saved for their poor clients $600,050 at a net cost of slightly less than that amount.[2] Cases in which benefits in cash or property are obtained are, of course, a minor part of the work of such organizations.

[1] Reginald Heber Smith: *Extending the Public Service of the Organized Bar through Legal Aid Work.*

[2] Emery A. Brownell: *Legal Aid*, Social Work Year Book, 1943 (U.S.A.).

Many important books and articles have been written by American students of legal aid, and the quantity of literature on the subject has in fact reached such proportions that the N.A.L.A.O. has published a *Tentative Bibliography of Material on Legal Aid Work* which runs to 250 pages. The same organization publishes a bi-monthly *Legal Aid News Letter* and the New York Legal Aid Society publishes the *Legal Aid Review* quarterly. The work has attracted some of the country's most distinguished lawyers and their writings and pronouncements are remarkable both for their vision and balanced judgment.

Considerable attention has also been paid to the client of small means, as distinct from the man who cannot afford to pay any fees at all, and the various schemes which have been evolved to meet this need are mentioned in Chapter XII.

A detailed description of the systems in further countries would be tedious and unnecessary, but it may be useful to note the way in which various points of general interest have been treated in different countries. An attempt has therefore been made to extract the relevant information and to present it in an easily digestible form in the following pages; further details and authority for the general statements made are given in Appendix B.*

The basis of the information is the report published by the League of Nations in 1927, entitled *Legal Aid for the Poor.* Wherever possible the information has been brought up to date, but time and war conditions have prevented this being done in every case. On the whole it is surprising how little the provisions have altered in the past, even when territory has changed hands, but, although the report is given in the present tense, it will be understood that, as regards some countries, it may be out of date. The form in which the various countries made their reports to the League has involved a certain amount of guesswork as to the practice on some points and the following analysis cannot claim to be absolutely accurate and comprehensive, but only to give a general picture of the situation.

No Legal Aid (1)

There is no legal aid (with the possible exception of legal aid in criminal matters) in China, Cuba, British Columbia, British

* Appendix B takes the place of Notes on the remainder of this Chapter and the small numerals refer to headings in Appendix B, under which further information will be found.

India and Panama. There are, in addition, some countries where the grant is extremely limited as, for example, in those British Dominions which have only the Common Law *in forma pauperis* procedure. Nevertheless it is true to say as is stated in the Introduction to the League of Nations Report: "(Legal Aid) facilities, in varying stages of development, appear indeed to be almost universal. The principle that it should not be impossible for the man without means to set in motion the machinery of justice is generally recognized".

Legal Advice (2)

Similarly there are very few countries where there is no legal advice obtainable. In practice wherever aid is given in litigation the authority which considers the application is almost bound to give a certain amount of advice when dealing with the application for aid and, in addition, in most countries where there is no official provision for advice, private bodies such as charitable societies, Trade Unions and the professional organizations of lawyers provide some measure of advice. In Belgium it is obligatory for each bar to provide at least one free consultation bureau. In Danzig, Finland, Sweden, Poland there are municipal bureaux, and in other countries the Ministry of Justice or some other Government Department maintains bureaux for advice.

Limitation of Legal Aid and Special Provisions.

It is very rare for the aid granted in litigation to be specifically limited to any particular types of case or to any particular courts. Some of the laws deliberately state that they apply to all courts, to appeals and to proceedings relating to the execution of judgments, but when this is not done it is often impossible to tell whether the provisions apply only to certain courts. In Italy and Belgium aid can be granted for proceedings before administrative tribunals as well as the courts.

There are certain types of proceedings which are usually dealt with by special provisions, for example, workmen's accidents, and in some of the States of the U.S.A., employment matters, small debts and matrimonial proceedings, as well as juvenile delinquency, are dealt with in special courts. In three Swiss cantons legal aid is not granted in defamation proceedings and, in one, there is no legal aid in divorce.

In only one case—Sweden—is there no condition that civil proceedings must appear to be well-founded before legal aid can be granted; the condition is not always stipulated but it is clear that if there was not a prima facie case the application would in practice be rejected.

Means (3)

The other almost universal condition of a grant is the poverty of the applicant. It is not always insisted upon in the case of criminal proceedings or workmen's accidents and there are a few other rare cases where poverty need not be shown. (3A)

In Denmark, for instance, in matrimonial cases and in suits in which heirs claim for a missing person's estate, the court is ordered, in the event of the defendant appearing without an advocate, to appoint one to represent him and, the Treasury pays the fees unless the plaintiff, having lost the action, is ordered to pay costs. In 1937 a similar provision was made in Norway so far as matrimonial proceedings are concerned, but in that country an advocate has to be appointed only if the defendant does not appear.

In Danzig the Legal Information Bureau has the duty of giving information and advice in matters concerning industrial and social legislation to any person domiciled or working in Danzig irrespective of their means.

Fixed Means Test (3B)

So far as the degree of poverty is concerned the outstanding fact is that a fixed monetary test, whether of capital or income is hardly ever found outside the British Empire ; Peru, Salvador, a few American States, and Spain are the only instances. The rule elsewhere is that the applicant must not be able to pay for the proceedings himself and Italy and Egypt specifically state that " the expression 'poverty' shall not be understood to mean complete destitution but a condition which renders the applicant incapable of bearing the costs of the action ". The Italian Decree specifies that applicants who are minors must also prove their parents' lack of means and wives their husbands' lack of means unless the parties are separated or it is a case where the husband is taking proceedings against the wife. In other cases the members of the family whose means must be taken into consideration are not specified but it may be assumed that not only the two relationships just mentioned are considered but any member of the family or household who is a dependant or a contributor and the test is frequently laid down as inability to pay " without encroaching upon the means necessary for the subsistence of himself or his family ".

It is usual to require more evidence as to the means of the applicant than his own statement, and this is most commonly done in the form of a certificate from some official. Sometimes the applicant's own statement is sufficient but the right to demand further evidence is reserved. Generally speaking applications can be made without any cost but in Italy a stamp of 6 lire has to be paid and in Spain if the application is rejected the applicant has to pay the costs of it.

Part Payment.

The aid given is not always entirely free. Part payment has been introduced in South Australia and in the scheme run by the College of Advocates, Buenos Aires, a contribution has to be made to the expenses of the bureau. The Belgian provision that a person who has some, but not sufficient, resources shall pay a sum fixed on the granting of the application has already been mentioned. In Germany in actions relating to property the grant has to state what part, if any, of the cost of the proceedings, the applicant can afford to pay. There is a provision for partial legal aid in the Polish Code of Civil Procedure, 1932, and the Model Regulations for Legal Advice Bureaux provide for legal services to be given free only to certain classes of people—small farmers and labourers, for example—prescribed fees being payable by others. In Spain the proportion of costs to be borne by persons of various elaborately defined categories is stipulated. In America a number of " reduced-fee " plans are in operation and some of these are described in Chapter XII.

The Certifying Authority (4)

In an overwhelming majority of countries the authority for the grant of legal aid is the Court. It is rare indeed for the grant or refusal of aid to be in the hands of members of the legal professions as in England ; in Western Australia and Tasmania the example of the mother country is followed, and Hungary, Roumania and San Marino are the only further examples which have been discovered. There are, of course, sometimes supplementary schemes run by the College of Advocates or similar bodies as independent charities, in which case the lawyers naturally have control and there are a few countries where the Government controls the grant of legal aid by leaving it in the hands of the Minister of Justice or other official. A number of instances were also given earlier of applications being dealt with by mixed commissions. These commissions are usually composed of advocates, judges or magistrates, and Government officials, but their authority is derived from the Court.

It is very rare for there to be no appeal against a refusal of legal aid and there is only one State—Tasmania—where the English system of applications being granted by practising lawyers has been adopted which does not allow an appeal.

Benefits of the Grant (5)

The benefits attached to a grant of legal aid now have to be considered.

Legal aid, with very few exceptions, involves the provision of an advocate, remission of court fees and exemption from giving security for costs. In certain of the lower courts an advocate may not be considered necessary but most courts have the power to provide representation.

Representation (5A)

It is difficult to tell from some of the reports whether or not the advocate of the poor person receives payment from the State. There is the clear case where representation is carried out by salaried lawyers and the converse case where the legal profession is under an " honourable obligation " to act in an honorary capacity. The latter clearly constitutes the largest class, but equally clearly the modern tendency is towards the introduction of payment for representation. As will be seen later the poor person's lawyer is not prevented from obtaining costs against the opposing party, so he will normally receive some payment if he is successful in the case. Sometimes rewards are offered for taking part in the honorary work of legal aid : in the State of Amazonas (Brazil) members of the commissions are given preference for appointment to any judicial office ; in Roumania probationers who take part may win a bonus awarded by the Order of Advocates for distinguished work.

Assistance with Out-of-Pocket Expenses (5B)

Another surprise to the lawyer brought up on the Poor Persons' Rules is the number of countries where the grant confers the right to have certain out-of-pocket expenses paid by the Treasury ; the list given in the Appendix is probably not complete but practically all the large countries are included. Amongst the items covered are witnesses' expenses, expert witnesses' fees and expenses, fares and subsistence allowances, the cost of copies of documents and of taking evidence on commission, postal charges, and the cost of inserting notices and advertisements in journals. It is sometimes required, as a safeguard against abuse, that the expenses should be certified as necessary and no doubt even when this is not stipulated the expenses are carefully scrutinized and only paid if they are reasonable.

Liability for Costs (6)

Another major topic is the question of costs. It appears to be universal in all countries apart from England and Tasmania for the liability of the opponent of the poor person to be unaffected by the fact that it is a poor person's suit and for costs to be awarded against him in the usual circumstances. Similarly costs can be awarded against the poor person in the ordinary way notwithstanding the grant of legal aid. In practice, of course, this liability will frequently be of no benefit to his opponent, or will be a serious hardship to the poor person, and some laws expressly limit the right to enforce the judgment as to costs.

On the other hand it is by no means certain that the poor person, even if successful in the proceedings, will recover the full amount of his costs from his opponent and in some circumstances, he may be liable to pay his own lawyers' and court fees. In South Australia the assisted person has to refund out-of-pocket expenses advanced to him, if he recovers money in the proceedings; in New South Wales he must pay all fees, charges, and solicitor and client costs up to one-quarter of the net amount recovered, providing it is over £50, and there is a similar provision in Western Australia and many other countries; in the Cantonal courts of Egypt he pays if he is successful in a claim of more than a certain amount. In some of the Brazilian States he has to pay a percentage of his winnings to his lawyer, in addition to the scale fee, as a reward for the successful free representation. In many other countries he is liable to pay fees and expenses if within a certain time he acquired sufficient resources, whether as a result of the proceedings or otherwise.

Legal Education.

Finally a study of foreign systems brings out the way in which legal aid can be used in the training of young lawyers, to the mutual advantage of students and applicants. The Legal Dispensaries run by the Glasgow University Law Society have already been noted, but very much more extensive work is done in Denmark. An article in the *Law Quarterly Review* of 1891 (7 *L.Q.R.*, 126) describes an excellent Legal Advice Centre at

Copenhagen, open all week, with four consulting rooms in each of which an advocate sits, with a student making notes of the case while the advocate handles the interview. The advocate and the student come on the same day each week so that old clients may see the same adviser if they come again. In 1890 there were 15,850 applications out of a population of 350,000 ; the Centre was opened in 1885. The organization spread to other towns, and in 1942 the Danish Student's Association's Office for Legal Aid dealt with 37,677 applications. The income limit is about £200 a year and there are about 70 lawyers and law students at the disposal of the bureau, assisted by about 70 undergraduates.

The College of Advocates at Buenos Aires runs a comprehensive scheme for legal advice and aid in which certain selected students not only sit with a member of the College when advising but take part in the conduct of cases which the Bureau fights on behalf of poor litigants when a settlement cannot be reached. In some of the American Universities, bureaux, known as Legal Aid Clinics, are run by professors and students as part of the regular course of legal training and some of them have attained a very high standard of development.

Further details of the use which has been made of legal aid in the education of lawyers would be premature. When, however, a legal aid system has been established which is worthy of the traditions of this country much benefit might be gained from a study of the experience of the Universities in America and elsewhere. For the time being, having concluded the historical and descriptive section of this book, the immediate task is to examine the defects which exist in the English provisions and to discuss practical measures of reform.

PART II

CRITICISM AND PROPOSALS

INTRODUCTORY NOTE TO PART II

Legal Aid is a single subject with many aspects. To separate the different aspects into chapters is bound to create arbitrary divisions and a somewhat arbitrary order in the arrangement of the topics. The order which has been adopted is as follows :

The first four of the following chapters are concerned with legal aid in litigation. The first three deal with the main criticisms of the Poor Persons' Rules of the High Court and the fourth with the provisions, or absence of provisions, in Courts other than the High Court. The next two chapters—XI and XII—are concerned with Legal Advice or Legal Aid Centres, first as regards advice, then as regards further action such as negotiation and litigation. Chapter XIII discusses the financial implications of the reforms which are necessary and Chapter XIV the question of the best organization to administer the legal aid scheme.

CHAPTER VII

THE APPLICATION FOR AID

It is not until he comes to study the systems of other countries that an English lawyer realizes that the system, whereby the legal profession, or one branch of it, decides whether a grant of legal aid shall be made or withheld, is open to question.

As we have seen, it is very rare indeed for practising lawyers to have this power: Hungary and Roumania appear to be the only examples on the Continent. An overwhelming majority of countries accepts the principle that the Court is the only proper authority for granting legal aid, although the power may be delegated to a judge or a mixed committee. In a few countries the State itself retains control of the grant and acts through the Minister of Justice or other legal official.

The reason for this difference from England is that abroad the principle has been recognized that legal aid is an essential part of the administration of justice and therefore should be dealt with by those who are primarily concerned with the administration of justice. Theoretically there can be no question that legal aid, without which access to the courts is in many cases barred, should be in the disposition of the courts of justice and not of advocates.

This was, of course, the case in England under the early Statutes, under the Rules of Court of 1883 and under the Poor Persons' Rules of 1914. It ceased to be so in High Court Proceedings when the Law Society made it known that the only way in which sufficient solicitors to conduct the cases could be obtained was to give them complete control of administration including the grant or refusal of certificates. In other words the fact that England has a scheme which depends upon the gratuitous services of the profession has resulted in solicitors having the right to decide whether or not they will give those gratuitous services in any particular case. The Poor Persons' Committees throughout the country are elected by the London and provincial Law Societies and their appointment is formally confirmed by the Lord Chancellor. They have the sole power in relation to the granting of Poor Persons' Certificates and there is no appeal against their decision.

Under the original Poor Persons' Rules the grant was actually made by the court after the case had been investigated by "Reporters" and there was a right of appeal by leave of the Judge in Chambers; the abolition of both these safeguards was soon the subject of a case in the Court of Appeal, Everett *v.* the Law Society,[1] on 21st June, 1926. According to the *Solicitors Journal*

Bankes L.J. went on to point out that the alterations in practice made by the new Rules were, whether by accident or design, of a most radical character and would, after this case, no doubt receive further careful consideration, and Atkin L.J. remarked upon the fact that nowhere in the Rules now obtaining were any regulations set forth determining or indicating in any way the manner in which the Committee, entrusted by the Law Society with this most important work, was to perform its duties. He confessed that it startled him to find that a non-judical body, from whose decision no appeal would lie, should have the power, as was here the case, to refuse an application by a person to sue *in forma pauperis*, without granting him an interview and without stating any reasons for their decision.

Whether or not the position received further consideration it was not altered and the only occasion on which the court has any say with regard to legal aid is when an application is made by a Poor Person for leave to appeal to the Court of Appeal.* It is still the practice, of the London Committee at least, to inform an applicant in a few lines that the application which he made months, or even years ago, has been rejected, and to give no reason for the decision except that if the case is considered to be one for the County Court and not the High Court a note is made to this effect. There is nothing more exasperating than to receive a blank refusal, especially after a long period of waiting, and nothing more calculated to cause excessive strictness in considering applications than the fact that there is no need to communicate any reason for the decision.

It has been argued that since solicitors bear the main burden of the procedure they are entitled to say what cases they shall accept. They are thus able to ensure that they are not compelled to undertake any unnecessary work. Solicitors will naturally want to keep down the volume of work as much as possible and they are, in fact, compelled to keep it down by the shortage of volunteers to conduct cases. Thus they are placed

[1] 70 *S.J.*, 745.

* No appeal is allowed by an admitted Poor Person without leave of the Court of Appeal, but if the party was not admitted as a Poor Person to take proceedings in the lower court his application is made to the Poor Persons' Committee in the usual way: O. xvi, rule 31 *E*.

in the position of having an interest in resisting any extension of the system,* however necessary, when they should be using the direct experience which they gain to point out extensions which are necessary. But solicitors are not the only people who are implicated. In the first place it is the duty of the State to see that all its citizens have adequate facilities for using the courts, and in the second place the public treasury bears the expenses of the administration of Poor Persons' Procedure and the court fees which are remitted when a certificate is granted.

Even if the Committees did not give way to the temptation which being sole judge in their own cause entails, it is a bad practice to allow it even to appear that they might not be impartial. Unfortunately it is clear that it is not just a question of appearances. While some Committees do all they can to help applicants, others are obviously unsympathetic. They complain of lack of gratitude on the part of applicants, of the way in which the application forms are filled in, of insufficient evidence having been collected by the applicant, and one Committe even alleged that applicants were waiting until they were unemployed so that they could bring divorce cases under the Rules. There are many ways in which an unsympathetic attitude leads to unfair decisions. One is through an over-strict interpretation of the financial limits, another is by taking the view that unless the applicant has been able himself to obtain all the necessary evidence, he has not shown a prima facie case, another is by considering the " worthiness " of an applicant. The last practice cannot be justified on any ground. It was foreshadowed by the 1925 Report, of which Judge Parry wrote, in his lively way :

> The Commission, however, agreed to two general principles. First, they acknowledged that it is " a proper function of the Government to ensure that meritorious poor persons are not deprived of access to the High Court by lack of means ". I do not like the word " meritorious ". I find no precedent for it in the Gospel. The word is not there. In my concordance I find " mercy " and then we go on to " merry ". I could understand suggesting " mercy " for the poor or proposing to make them " merry ". But the word " meritorious " I find indigestible. I know of no Order of Merit for the poor. Mr. Justice P. O. Lawrence, the Chairman of the Commission, must have had a reason for proposing that only the meritorious poor should have legal aid The word suggests " Sandford and Merton " and Miss Edgeworth and " Ministering Children " rather than divorce procedure. But it may

* This does not mean that they have always followed their own interests. As the previous Chapter and other references show, some committees have stressed the need for reforms and have voluntarily undertaken further burdens.

be a term of art in the Chancery Division, the effect of which I do not appreciate. For the purpose of my argument I must with all respect strike the word out as embarrassing and irrelevant to the statement of the principle.

And the second principle that the Commission lays down in unequivocal language is " that there exists a moral obligation on the part of the profession, in return for the monopoly in the practice of the law which it enjoys, to render gratuitous legal assistance to those members of the community who cannot afford to pay for such assistance ". Here again I have cut out a proviso " that no undue burden is thereby cast on any individual members of the profession ". This phrase should be quashed for uncertainty, as the old criminal pleader would say. But the two principles as I have amended them are really excellent. Left as they were originally drafted, an attorney is invited to say to the poor man who asks assistance : " My good man, you do not seem to me meritorious and even if you are I am far too tired to attend to you." I am sure this was not intended and I am equally sure the profession do not want these qualifying phrases and will accept the principles in their integrity.

The profession did accept the principles but they were soon forgotten, and we find a surprising number of Poor Persons' Committees reporting that they confine their assistance to " deserving applicants " or people of " deserving character ".* One Committee ingenuously claims that they " usually give the applicant the benefit of any doubt on the point of character ".[1] The Report on Poor Persons' Procedure for 1936 reveals the astounding fact that some members of committees consider it their duty to save the Divorce Court judges from granting divorces too easily—" One of the Honorary Secretaries (of the provincial committees) volunteers his personal opinion that it is so easy for a petitioner in an undefended divorce case to obtain a decree that, if the chance of success and not the merit of the applicant were taken as the test, help would be given to the wrong people."

The committees are placed in a most difficult position by their practice of usurping the Divorce Court's function of deciding " discretion cases ". As most readers will know, where the Petitioner himself has committed adultery, he is obliged to disclose this fact to the Court which then has a discretion whether to grant a divorce to the Petitioner, or, on a cross-petition, to the Respondent, or to both, or to neither. The practice of the

* Some allowance must be made for the fact that the reports of Poor Persons' Committees are intended for solicitors. The Honorary Secretaries are tempted to stress the good character of all the applicants who are accepted in order to encourage solicitors to join the rotas.

[1] Annual Report, 1930.

Divorce Courts varies widely from time to time and there was recently a comprehensive statement on the position by the President of the Probate, Divorce and Admiralty Division, drawing attention to the variety of choices which a Judge has in these cases and the freedom of his discretion. It is almost impossible in a particular case to say that the Judge definitely will not give the applicant any relief and the difficulty of the decision is one of the strong arguments used against giving County Court judges jurisdiction in divorce. Yet when one of the provincial committees raised this point the query was published in the Law Society's Annual Report of 1929 with a note, "The committee are entitled to exercise their discretion as to whether or not the misconduct is of such a nature as to induce the court to refuse to grant him relief." But some committees would like to go further and to refuse relief even when the court would grant it. "The parties," says one Committee, "have obviously regarded the marriage so lightly that it has felt reluctant to put the court and the conducting solicitor to so much trouble in bringing about its dissolution." * When a shortage of conducting solicitors again became acute with the outbreak of war there was, as the annual report observed, an increase in the proportion of rejected applications in respect of discretionary cases, and in the 1942 report there is a noticeable increase in the emphasis on the worthiness and the deserts of applicants.

Thus the jealously safeguarded discretion of the Divorce Court Judges is not only being exercised by committees of the Law Societies, so far as poor persons are concerned, but is being exercised on grounds of professional expediency instead of on those general principles of public policy which are the basis of the discretion rule.

This is only one difficulty; another is the practice of refusing a certificate because the case is one which could be brought in the County Court. There are some cases of this kind which, in private practice, would nevertheless be commenced in the High Court; from the point of view of relieving the Poor Persons' rotas, however, there is an obvious temptation to reject all such applications, since solicitors are under no obligation to provide free representation in the County Court. There are other types of actions which are very unlikely to be accepted; defamation

* Quoted by "Barrister" who also cites another committee which "admits that it does not 'encourage' applications by persons who have themselves committed, or are living in, adultery, and refers to cases in which they have granted certificates where there were 'extenuating circumstances'".

proceedings, for example, may mean a great deal to the applicant who has been libelled or slandered, and cannot be brought in the County Court, but such an action will probably appear troublesome and unnecessary to a committee which knows there is little prospect of damages being recovered. Again it is a very difficult position for a committee when an applicant wishes to bring an action against a solicitor or other local person. These are only extreme instances of the undesirability of any non-judicial body exercising the power to grant legal aid.

This question of the authority to grant certificates has been very fully considered by Dr. Cohn. He points out that there are three separate systems found in different countries :

1. The certifying authority is the body of advocates or a commission * containing advocates. This he describes as the oldest system.
2. The grant is made by an administrative authority, such as the Minister of Justice.
3. The grant is made by the Court itself, normally the Court which will try the action.

Dr. Cohn is wholly opposed to the first system :

> Legal aid is not a favour bestowed upon a poor applicant by the members of the Bar. It is—or at least it should by now be—a right granted to him by the State as part of the protection which the State bestows upon its citizens. There is therefore no reason why the decision upon applications for the grant of legal aid should rest in the hands of professional bodies. . . . The rejection of the application for the grant of legal aid is in the nature of things in most cases tantamount to a dismissal of the action—not in law, of course, but in fact. In the overwhelming majority of cases a poor applicant who has not succeeded in obtaining legal aid will not be able to enforce his rights in court at all. The decision about his application should therefore be surrounded by no less strict guarantees for the impartiality and quality of the body deciding about it than is any ordinary action itself. . . . The choice would therefore seem to lie between leaving the decision to administrative authorities and leaving it to the law courts.[1]

And as there are no suitable administrative authorities in this country Dr. Cohn concludes that the decision must be left to the Courts. While it would no doubt be possible for the Lord Chancellor's Department or the Attorney-General's office to act

* I consider it is misleading to include the commissions under the first system ; even when they are composed entirely of practising lawyers, as in Scotland, they are merely acting as agents for the court (or in the case of Haiti of the Ministry of Justice).

[1] 59 *L.Q.R.*, 265, 266.

in this capacity such an arrangement would not be as desirable as to leave it in the hands of the courts. The objections to this are that it would throw a considerable burden on the courts and that the same Judge would have to deal twice with the same set of facts. For this reason, in Scotland applications are considered by Reporters on *Probabilis Causa* before they are presented to the Court for formal decision and the Scottish Committee proposes [1] that the decision itself should be left to the Reporters, in the Sheriff Courts, subject, however, to an appeal to the Sheriff-Substitute. Dr. Cohn deals with the difficulty in another way by recommending that the Master in the Supreme Court and the Registrar in the County Courts should be entrusted with the decision, subject to an appeal to the Judge. This would involve an increase in the number of Masters and Registrars and possibly the appointment of special poor persons' Masters for the purpose.

The Haldane Society * has accepted Dr. Cohn's arguments and has suggested that the Clerk to Justices should act for the Police Court and the Clerk of the Peace and Clerk of Assize for Quarter Sessions and the Assize Courts. The only objection that might be taken to the proposal is that it is hardly desirable to have so many certifying authorities as would be involved in having a separate authority for each separate court throughout the country. Dr. Cohn's suggestion of special poor persons' Masters opens up the possibility of having in each district one or more of these specialists on court proceedings to decide applications for all the local courts, with or without co-option of experts from the particular court concerned. Only by some such means could a reasonable uniformity in the grant of certificates be obtained. The Haldane Society would also allow their proposed Legal Aid Bureaux to grant certificates where they had failed to achieve a settlement, but this would give the Bureaux unwarranted power and, while their recommendation should carry considerable weight, the actual decision should not be left in their hands.

There is no reason, however, why the court should not choose persons other than the Master or Registrar to deal with applications.† So long as the authority is derived from the court, and

[1] Cmd. 5435, para. 42.

* It should be made clear that the Haldane Society is responsible for two different sets of proposals. Its original proposals are contained in *The Law and Reconstruction*; these are criticized by Dr. Cohn in his article and the Society's new proposals follow fairly closely Dr. Cohn's recommendations.

† As for example, committees of the Law Societies or of the organizations controlling the legal aid scheme, if different from the Law Society.

there is a right of appeal to the court, it does not matter what agency is employed to do the routine work provided it is competent. But it is important, as the foregoing observations have shown, that the court should have the power to supervise a function which is essentially the first stage in court proceedings.

The certifying authority would have the duty of deciding whether the applicant's means entitled him to assistance and whether he had reasonable grounds for taking legal proceedings. Legal Aid Bureaux would be able to help in both these matters and possibly a certificate from the Inspector of Taxes or Social Welfare Officer could be supplied with regard to income. It is easy to imagine the considerations which led Sweden to dispense with the requirement that reasonable grounds for the proceedings must be shown, but the question is merely one of defining the meaning of " reasonable ". It is submitted that there are no grounds for making the standard higher in a poor person's case than in any other. Public policy demands that certain actions should not be tolerated by the courts whether the parties are poor persons or not and, just as an action can be dismissed if it is frivolous or vexatious, or if no reasonable cause of action has been disclosed,[1] an application for aid by a poor person should be rejected on these, and on no other, grounds. The decisions which have already been given on these points would thus be available for the guidance of the certifying authority.

Dr. Cohn is opposed to the practice, found in several foreign countries, of allowing the applicant's opponent to appear before the certifying authority, for the reason that the proceedings tend to become cumbersome and are hardly more effective than the appearance of the applicant alone.[2] It is true that such proceedings may amount to something in the nature of a preliminary trial but there is no objection to that on principle since the issue is different from the issue to be decided on the actual hearing of the case ; it is comparable with the preliminary examination of a prisoner before a magistrate. A certain amount of time may be wasted in some cases but that would be more than counterbalanced in others by the enormous amount of time saved to far more people by preventing an unnecessary case from going ahead. It might be said that the hearing of the opponent is unnecessary because he can apply, after the action has been commenced, to strike it out if it is frivolous or vexatious or if no cause of action is

[1] O. xxv, rule 4.

[2] 59 *L.Q.R.*, 364.

disclosed and he can also apply under O. XVI, rule 29, which says: "The Court or a Judge may at any time (and whether or not any application be made by any Law Society or by any other person for that purpose) discharge the certificate. . . ." The applications are made to the Master, with a right of appeal to the Judge in Chambers and to the Court of Appeal and the disadvantage is that they can only be made when solicitors have been allotted and have done a considerable amount of work.

It is true that the Scottish Committee appears to recommend that, in the case of the Sheriff Courts at least, the right of the opponent to be heard should be abolished, except where he also is applying for admission to the Poor's Roll. But the consequences to the opponent must be given full consideration. If he is unsuccessful he has no complaint against the system, but if he is successful he will very probably have to pay his own costs although he has been proved to be in the right. It is possible that if he were given the opportunity he would be able to prove to the certifying authority that the applicant had undisclosed means or to reveal some fact that would completely alter the decision. The fact that he cannot do so at present under the Poor Persons' Rules is a source of grievance to the few people who have suffered a barren success against a poor person. Professor Maguire has pointed out [1] how *in forma pauperis* procedure fell into disrepute because it was abused and Mr. Mullins was more impressed with the hardships of poor persons' opponents than those of the poor persons themselves.[2] The latter suggests that the opponent should have the right to oppose the application both as to means and as to the merits of the case. He also suggests that in any case where the plaintiff cannot pay the costs of the action or give adequate security for the defendant's costs the defendant should have the option of having his case tried by conciliation methods, whatever the amount of the claim. This would involve "abandonment of the rules of evidence, the possibility of trial on documents alone, or the hearing of witnesses at different times without cross-examination by the parties". This directly conflicts with the principle that a person should not be forced by lack of means to accept any system of justice which is not considered to be the best. Nevertheless it cannot be stressed too much that every attempt at conciliation is desirable and conciliatory tribunals have been tried with success in Norway and

[1] 36 *Harvard Law Review*, 361 ff.; 156 *L.T.*, 345–9 and 368–70.
[2] *In Quest of Justice*, Chap. XIX.

Denmark, and in France, where there is a Juge de Paix, whose function has been described as not so much to try actions as to endeavour to prevent them.[1] On the other hand they have not proved successful up to the present in America and there seems little prospect of conciliation tribunals as such being instituted here in the near future. It is, however, to be hoped that every opportunity for conciliation will be afforded in the course of a poor person's application for aid, and this can only be done if the opponent has an opportunity of being heard.

[1] M. Poincaré: *How France is Governed*, quoted by Mr. Mullins.

CHAPTER VIII

THE MEANS TEST AND THE PROVISION OF OUT-OF-POCKET EXPENSES

Few people will consider that the present income limits under the Poor Persons' Rules—£2 a week or, in special circumstances, £4 a week—are sufficiently high in 1944 to cover all persons who are prevented by lack of means from bringing legal proceedings in the High Court, or for that matter the County Court. This income limit was fixed in 1921 as a result of the recommendations of the first Lawrence Committee.[1] Previously there had only been a capital test and more cases had been accepted than there were solicitors to conduct them.

Obviously our conception of what constitutes a poor person has grown harsher in the last twenty odd years; as early as 1925 the *Law Journal* wrote [2] "the present limit of means is, in these days of high wages particularly, fixed so low as to exclude a very large class of persons who cannot bring themselves within such a limit, and yet to whom the cost of even an undefended divorce suit is almost prohibitive". Certainly before 1929 the London and some of the provincial Committees [3] had recognized the fact that the lower limit was out of date and were accepting applicants without dependants if they had not more than £3 a week, the cost of living being considered sufficient "special circumstances". Since 1921 the cost of living has increased greatly and Sir William Beveridge states [4] that between 1938 and 1943 alone it has increased by about 30 per cent. In other matters some allowance has been made for this fact. There have been two increases in Workmen's Compensation allowances, an extension of National Health Insurance, increased pay for serving men and civil defence workers, supplementary pensions, war bonuses and a general increase in wages, including the fees of solicitors, but no increase in the Poor Persons' limits has been made and for the simple reason that the rotas of solicitors are not adequate to cope with the increase in cases which would result.

[1] Cmd. 430. [2] 60 *L.J.*, 213 ff., 237 ff., and 261 ff.

[3] Law Society's Annual Report, 1929: Note attached to the Northamptonshire Committee's Report.

[4] *Social Insurance and Allied Services*, Cmd. 6404.

An applicant must still have less than £3 a week, even in London, unless he can show special circumstances and the rules do not make any provision for his liabilities in the way of dependants or otherwise except by means of the margin between cases which require special circumstances and those which do not, a margin which should long since have been absorbed by the increase in the cost of living. A man may have fourteen dependant children but if his " normal income " is a penny more than £4 a week he is excluded from the provisions and is liable to pay the same court fees, expenses and professional fees as the wealthiest man. It is as clear a case of justice being denied to the poor as there could be.

In addition to the income test the applicant must show that he does not possess capital assets worth more than £50, or, in special circumstances, £100, excluding his clothes, tools of his trade, and the subject matter of the proceedings. These are the limits which were fixed in 1914. There is no provision that the assets must be readily realizable : if he has furniture, or a house on a Building Society mortgage, he is presumably expected to execute a Bill of Sale or a second mortgage to pay for his action. If he has been thrifty enough to save £50 or £100 he is penalized for his thrift and must risk his savings in paying his own and possibly his opponent's costs.

Except in one special case the Rules do not require the means of any person other than the applicant to be taken into account but many of the provincial committees feel strongly about anyone being granted a certificate if he has relations who could afford to pay for the case in the ordinary way, and make a practice of excluding any applicants whom they find to be in this position. This practice received official encouragement from the London Committee, which reported in 1940 that a Judge had commented adversely on a Poor Person's certificate being issued when the applicant's father could well have paid the costs, and recommended that committees should, therefore, take into account the means of the immediate family of the applicant. Presumably the applicant in the case quoted was not an infant because where an infant is suing by his " next friend " the Committees need to be satisfied that the next friend is a poor person. It is perfectly reasonable that they should do so ; perfectly reasonable also that the means of the husband or wife of an applicant should be taken into account, but in fact the Rules only stipulate that this shall be done in the case of a wife who is a petitioner in a matrimonial suit [1] and who can, therefore, apply to court for an order that her husband shall pay her costs up to the setting down of the action and provide security for her further costs. Anything in the nature of a family means test is studiously avoided in the Rules. If this is to be altered, and there is much to be said in favour of the means of a husband being considered in actions other than divorce, the point should be specifically dealt with in the Rules. At present the forms of application do not ask for particulars of the means of relations and have no right to do so. If such matters are to be taken into account the financial limits should be appropriately increased.

In the special case mentioned above, where a wife is a petitioner in matrimonial proceedings, the qualification for a certificate is that either the means of the husband and wife must be within the usual limits or it must be reasonable for a certificate to be granted. The latter alternative, whereby a certificate may be granted if it is reasonable, irrespective of means, is the one case in the Poor Persons' Rules in which a fixed means test does not have to be applied. This lack of pliability has been strongly criticized on the ground that the requirement that an applicant's means must be below a certain amount excludes a multitude of considerations which affect the value of a man's capital and income.[2] Poverty, like so many other things, is relative. It is quite clear, for example, that a person is poor from the point of view of legal aid, who is not poor from the point of view of public assistance, and again, a person may be perfectly able to take certain kinds of legal action but may have far too little money when it comes to proceedings of a different sort; and an applicant who has heavy responsibilities and commitments is in a very different position from the man with none.

The allowance of twice the amount of capital and income if "special circumstances" can be shown is, of course, intended to overcome these difficulties but it is very doubtful whether this arrangement is sufficiently elastic. It is significant that hardly any of the foreign countries attempt to lay down a financial limit and the one notable exception, Spain, deals with the point at tremendous length but still does not cover all the possibilities and leaves a certain amount to the discretion of the judge.[3]

[1] O. xvi, rule 23.
[2] E. J. Cohn, 59 *L.Q.R.*, 271; Law Society's Annual Reports, particularly 1932, p. 136.
[3] *L.*, 227, quoted by E. J. Cohn, 59 *L.Q.R.*, 359, 360.

In America forty-one of the States had no fixed test according to a report of 1936 and the National Association of Legal Aid Organizations points out that circumstances completely alter cases and that the wrong man will always find a way to beat tests. Even in our own criminal provisions the matter is left to the discretion of the court. The Finlay Committee considered this question of the degree of poverty which should entitle a prisoner to legal aid and reported : [1]

> No exact rule has so far been laid down, and we recommend that it is better not to attempt a definition. We think that it is better to leave the matter to the discretion of the authority granting legal aid. If the suggestions which we have made earlier in this Report lead to legal aid being more frequently granted by committing justices, that will, from this point of view, be all to the good ; for the justices with their knowledge of local conditions and with their facilities for making any necessary enquiries are peculiarly qualified to deal with the matter.

The Scottish Committee also reported [2] against any fixed rule as to means being laid down.

The abolition of fixed limits in civil cases would not of itself, secure a more generous consideration of means. Both the State and the legal profession have a financial interest in as few poor persons being admitted as possible and a case was quoted by the Scottish Committee where a certificate of poverty was refused to a woman with eleven children whose husband was receiving 45*s*. a week.[3] The true basis of any test should be, as it is in the great majority of countries, whether the applicant can afford to bring the necessary legal proceedings. The certifying authority will, however, have to adopt some general standard and a certain degree of uniformity throughout the country is desirable. Any sum which may be stipulated is, of course, liable to become out of date but it would save a great many hopeless applications being made, as well as provide a safeguard against excessive severity, if a figure was made known as the standard for a normal case, due allowance being made for dependants. In any event the certifying authority should be given a wide discretion to cover cases where the cost of proceedings is likely to be particularly high or where commitments are exceptionally heavy.

Under the present procedure the applicant has to make a statutory declaration as to his means and case. The form is inevitably complicated and it is practically always necessary for

[1] Cmd. 2638, para. 20. [2] Cmd. 5435, para. 43.
[3] Ibid., para. 29.

somebody, usually the secretary of the Poor Persons' Committee, to assist in filling it in after the necessary information has been obtained. If, after the grant of a certificate, the assisted person ceases to be a poor person, he must inform the conducting solicitor who informs the Poor Persons' Committee. The ascertainment of means could be made easier and more reliable if the common practice of a certificate as to means by some official were adopted. The Public Assistance or Social Welfare Officer does this in Scotland and he, or preferably the Inspector of Taxes, could no doubt carry out the same function in this country. But, as the Scottish Committee has recommended,[1] the decision as to whether the applicant's means entitle him to legal aid should not rest with this official. So far as legal *advice* is concerned the financial qualification should be a very general one and the applicant's own statement should be accepted without further evidence. It might even be advisable, as is often done in practice, to leave the whole matter to the applicant's honesty without requiring a written statement. Social workers have little faith in declarations : they are only necessary for a few people and these are just the people who will have no scruples about making a false declaration ; very little is lost if one interview is given free to an applicant who is not entitled to it and the true position will usually be discovered before long. Moreover, it is a fact that most working class wives do not know how much their husbands earn. The great temptation at present as regards obtaining both legal advice and legal aid in the High Court, is the fact that no assistance at all is available if the application is rejected. Poor people do not, as a rule, want to get something for nothing ; they are often anxious to pay for the assistance they receive and make substantial voluntary contributions to Poor Man's Lawyers funds where these are accepted ; it is when they are told that they are not poor enough to get assistance on any feasible terms that they are tempted to falsify their statements.

This leads us to the question of payment of reduced fees. Clearly the financial limits now in force are very much less generous than they were when they were originally fixed and the qualification for completely free proceedings ought to be raised, but the hardship is made all the more acute by the fact that there is a hard and fast line between those who qualify as poor persons, and who are liable for no fees or costs, and those who

[1] Cmd. 5435, paras. 29, 42 and 43.

do not qualify and who are liable for full fees and costs. This difficulty is stressed in the Law Society's Report for 1942 where it is pointed out that the increase in wages is taking many people outside the Rules—" the result is there is becoming a large class of persons whose means are just in excess of the Poor Persons' limits, but who are scarcely in a position to afford full scale charges for the legal assistance which they require ". Even a straightforward undefended divorce costs £50, £60 or £70 and any complication increases the cost; a nullity suit, defended divorce, accident or other case may cost many hundreds of pounds.* It is useless to ignore the high cost of legal proceedings. In Mr. Mullins' book *In Quest of Justice* descriptions will be found [1] of many cases of a type which a person of moderate means might wish to bring where the costs would be quite outside his reach. Such a person, if he cannot obtain a Poor Persons' certificate is completely helpless under the existing system, but he could afford to pay something towards his case and it is very desirable that if he could, he should, not only because it saves other people paying for him but because he is subject to the same deterrent as other litigants and will have a financial interest in keeping the costs of his case as low as possible.

The proposal that there should be part payment in these cases has frequently been made by Poor Persons' Committees [2] and has been carried into practice by some. In York, for example, the solicitors on the rota will conduct divorce cases for £30 in appropriate circumstances and they also give assistance at reduced fees in affiliation cases. The practice is not uncommon on the Continent and in America. It has been recommended by the Scottish Committee [3] and it has been adopted in the scheme formulated by the Law Society for the benefit of Citizens' Advice Bureaux. There has been some opposition

* R. M. Jackson in *The Machinery of Justice in England* gives the following as a fair example of the Plaintiff's Costs in an ordinary action in the High Court:

		Solicitor and Client	Party and Party
		£	£
Solicitors' charges		80	60
Disbursements:	Court Fees	30	30
	Payment to witnesses	50	20
	Counsel's Fees	70	36
	Miscellaneous	10	5
		240	150

[1] E.g., p. 36 ff., p. 203 ff.
[2] See, for example, Annual Reports 1932, 136; 1938, 140.
[3] Cmd. 5435, para. 43.

to the proposal in the legal profession although it was recommended for divorce cases as long ago as 1925 by the *Law Journal* [1] and has received support from many quarters in recent years. The opposition is growing less and in any event the fact remains that some assistance must be given to the person of small means if justice is to be made available to him and, if he can afford to make some payment for the assistance, everything is in favour of his doing so.

So far we have been concerned in this chapter with the person who is considered too wealthy for the benefit of the Poor Persons' Rules, now we have to consider the person who is too poor to take advantage of them. Gurney Champion was not exaggerating when he described the Rules as creating a privileged class of poor person, sandwiched between those who had just too much money to obtain a certificate and those who were so poor that when they obtained a certificate they could not provide sufficient money for the out-of-pocket expenses of their case.

As has been stated earlier it was originally intended that the Treasury should provide a fund out of which necessary disbursements could be paid. When that did not materialize there was a project to raise the money by an appeal to the public and the *Law Journal* wrote: [2] "Meanwhile the urgent thing is the creation of a fund out of which the out-of-pocket expenses of solicitors are to be payable. The whole success of the system, indeed, depends upon it, since solicitors, however willing to give their services gratuitously, cannot be expected to loosen their own purse strings to pay for the travelling of witnesses and copying of documents." But this fund has not been formed to this day. It might be possible to absolve the Government from the charge of complete indifference as to whether poverty prevents a citizen getting legal justice, if it were not for the findings of the Lawrence Committees. Those have already been fully described: they show that inability to pay the disbursements was the cause of a large proportion of poor persons' cases not being proceeded with. Year after year some of the Poor Persons' Committees have testified to the same effect.

The present position is that before a poor person's case can be started he has to pay a deposit of, usually, £5. The absurdity of this requirement in some cases is unconsciously revealed by the report of one committee in 1931:

[1] 60 *L.J.*, 213 ff., 237 ff. and 261 ff.

[2] 49 *L.J.*, 362.

> My committee do not grant certificates in cases where the joint means of the husband and wife exceed £2 per week unless there really are exceptional circumstances, nor in any case where they know that the applicant's relatives are in a position to provide the money to pay the costs in the ordinary way. We have, however, noticed that in spite of all our care, applicants who have sworn that they have no means, etc., pay the £5 deposit remarkably soon after it is required.

In many cases, as was found by Scottish Committee,[1] the money is raised by pawning and borrowing, sometimes at exorbitant rates of interest. It is little wonder that poor persons do not always appear sufficiently grateful for the charity they are receiving. Numerous appeals for help are made to organizations such as the Charity Organization Society, which has had to make a practice of providing deposits only in those divorce cases where incest is involved. Often the money cannot be found at all: the Berks, Bucks and Oxfordshire Law Society reported in 1928 that out of a total of twenty-seven applicants in one year, six had to be rejected because the applicants could not pay the preliminary deposit. Incidentally this is all the more unfortunate because the full amount of the deposit which the committees demand is not always used. The sums representing deposits which have not been reclaimed amount to several thousands of pounds and an article published in 1938 [2] records that the Manchester Committee alone held £500 representing unclaimed deposits.

The cost of proceedings to a poor person does not always stop at £5. The first Lawrence Report [3] gives £20 as the actual out-of-pocket expenses of a nullity suit and there are many actions of a different kind in which this sum would be equalled or exceeded. Nor is the amount of the deposit the only expense to which the poor person is put; he has his own travelling and subsistence expenses and loss of wages to consider and in a divorce suit he may be ordered to pay his wife's costs up to the setting down of the action and provide security for her future costs, in addition, possibly, to paying her alimony.

The most common expense which has to be met is with regard to the production of evidence. As a special committee appointed by the International Law Association said in 1903, " It is patent that if a pauper cannot get his testimony, he will in most cases lose his cause, and he may not be able to get it without paying for it ", and the American Bar Association's Standing Committee

[1] Cmd. 5435, para. 17. [2] 186 *L.T.*, 296. [3] Cmd. 430.

on Legal Aid Work was referring to witness fees and newspaper notices when it stated in its 1941 Report, " It is the experience of every legal aid organization that frequently the amount of such fees and expenses is so great that the poor simply must go without redress." This is fully corroborated by the experience of Poor Man's Lawyer Associations in this country, some of which have established Cases Funds with which to assist County Court cases, for the problem is not confined to the High Court.

The London Poor Persons' Committee and some other committees have done all they can to remove this hardship by constantly appealing to the charity of experts and others who would normally charge a fee for their services. They succeeded in persuading some newspapers to accept Legal Notices at a very reduced charge, until the war put a stop to this ; they persuaded some of the doctors who carry out medical examinations in nullity suits to act free of charge ; they found legal photographers and, through the Automobile Association, an engineer, to give assistance and expert evidence in particular cases ; arrangements were made whereby in some districts Police evidence could be obtained free and the attendance of Police Officers secured without charge except for out-of-pocket expenses ; local authorities were advised by their Association to reduce the fees payable to official witnesses, the Admiralty agreed to waive their claim to the pay of an officer who attends as a witness, providing a substitute could be found and the witness's out-of-pocket expenses paid. The Surveyors' Institute and probation officers rendered assistance from time to time.

One has to be grateful that so much has been done but by no means the whole field has been covered. One point which deserves special mention is the difficulty and expense of collecting evidence, particularly in divorce cases. Poor Persons' Committees frequently complain that applicants appear to confuse the functions of a solicitor with those of an enquiry agent and Poor Man's Lawyers have the same experience. But what is the applicant to do ? It is simply ironical to tell a woman who cannot leave her children or a man who cannot leave his work that they must either travel to some part of the country themselves and find the necessary witnesses or they must pay enquiry agents' fees. In accident cases, too, it may be impossible to know whether or not the claim is sufficiently strong for further action until an experienced investigator has been sent to interview a witness personally. Then there are cases where a doctor, perhaps a specialist, will have to travel to Assizes to give evidence, or where a chemist is needed to make experiments, or where plans, models, photographs and translations have to be prepared.

The miscellaneous arrangements which have been made for reducing the expenses of poor persons' cases seldom apply to the whole country nor do they cover all the points which may be involved in a case. The fact that such efforts have been made by the committees and that Cases Funds have been formed by Poor Man's Lawyer Associations shows that there is a need, and it is obviously one which cannot adequately be met by depending upon the charitable response of numerous different persons and bodies. Access to the courts will be unfairly impeded until official arrangements are made for providing the incidental services necessary for the presentation of a case and for providing funds for other out-of-pocket expenses. A glance at Appendix B will show how widely this has been done in other countries for many years past ; it is done to some extent in the criminal provisions of this country, where the solicitor may be allowed any out-of-pocket expenses actually and reasonably incurred ; it was considered a fundamental factor in the working of the Poor Persons' Rules when they were first formulated in 1912 ; the time has surely come for action to be taken.

CHAPTER IX

LIABILITY FOR COSTS

There is one further matter in connection with litigation which will become of major importance if, as is hoped, legal aid becomes available in more cases, that is, the liability of the poor person and his opponent for costs.

Under the present rules the position is that, unless the court or judge otherwise orders, neither the poor person nor his opponent receives costs from, or pays costs to, the other party.

The court or judge may order the opponent to pay—

(1) the poor person's out-of-pocket expenses, but not office expenses or counsel's or court fees, and

(2) if the opponent has acted unreasonably in bringing or defending the suit, or if special circumstances require it, the opponent may be ordered to pay the poor person's costs and profit costs but not counsel's fees or court fees;

(3) in a case of unusual length or difficulty the opponent may be ordered to pay the poor person's solicitor a sum in addition to out-of-pocket expenses.

All out-of-pocket expenses and other costs are to be taxed and enforcement of the order cannot be carried out without the leave of the court; the court is not to grant leave unless it is satisfied that the opponent has the means to pay.

So far as the poor person is concerned he can be made liable for his opponent's costs only if he has obtained a certificate by fraud or misrepresentation. He is not liable to pay costs to his own solicitors, except that when he has recovered property he may be ordered to pay the amount of his solicitor and client costs, or a smaller sum, up to one quarter of the value of the property recovered, less disbursements.

The rule that the opponent of a poor person shall not normally pay any costs even when he loses the case, is not found in any other State except Tasmania, where the English Rules have been copied. Its history in England is interesting.

The statute 11 Henry VII c. 12 provided that a poor person could bring an action and be represented without charge, but a practice grew up of charging him court fees and fees for counsel and attorney if he recovered more than £5, the theory being that he then ceased to be a pauper and was, therefore, no longer within the terms of the Act. The costs which the poor person thus had to pay could be recovered from an opponent who had been ordered to pay costs.

In the opinion of many lawyers this was an unlawful practice —the payments made by the poor person were merely donations and it was wrong for the opponent to be made liable for donations which the poor person chose to make. In order to stop this, Rule 121 of Hilary Term of 1853 provided that " no fees shall be payable by a pauper to his counsel and attorney . . . by reason of a verdict being found for such pauper exceeding £5 " and Rule 28 of Trinity Term of 1853 provided " a person admitted to sue *in forma pauperis* shall not in any case be entitled to costs from the opposite party, unless by order of the court or a judge ".

The statute did not apply to the Chancery Courts, which, however, adopted its provisions so far as they considered it satisfied the requirements of justice. These courts did not take the same view of the opponent's immunity from costs but in many cases held him liable for " Dives costs ", that is, any payments actually made by the poor person, even if not legally due. In Scatchmer *v.* Foulkard [1] Lord Somers ordered a pauper " his costs like other suitors, for, though he is at no costs, or but small costs, yet the counsel and clerks do not give their labour to the defendant but to the pauper ". In Rubery *v.* Morris (1849) [2] Lord Cottenham observed that it appears " to be most consistent with principle and most reconcilable with the weight of authority to hold that any party asserting an unfounded claim by bill, or resisting a well-founded claim by answer, should not profit by the poverty of his opponent, but should, upon failure, pay the ordinary costs of the litigation ". And Order XL, rule 5 (1849), provided " where costs are ordered to be paid to a party suing or defending *in forma pauperis* such costs shall be taxed as Dives Costs unless the Court shall otherwise direct ".

The independence of Chancery practice was abolished by the *Judicature Act* but the Rules of Court 1883 left this point doubtful. Order XVI, rule 31, provided that costs, unless the Court or Judge otherwise directed, were to be taxed as in other cases, but in Carson *v.* Pickersgill,[3] where the above history was reviewed, the Court of Appeal held that, taken in conjunction with the other rules, this meant that a poor person could only recover the costs he had paid or was liable to pay, that is to say

[1] 1 Eq. Ca. Abr., 125.
[2] 1 Mac. and G., 413.
[3] 1885, 54 *L.J.Q.B.*, 484.

"costs out of pocket" by which the Court meant not only cash payments but also sums due in respect of the employment of clerks on the case.

This was the interpretation which was put on the new rules which came into force in 1914 so that what the 1925 Committee called "office expenses" were allowed until that Committee secured their abolition in 1926. From that date the general rule was that no costs were payable in a poor person's suit apart from the poor person's out-of-pocket expenses, but the judge had a general discretion to depart from this rule. The principles governing the exercise of this discretion, enumerated at the beginning of this chapter, came into force in January 1935 as a result of the report of a committee appointed by the Supreme Court Rules Committee.[1] The committee were opposed to any fundamental change but thought that the circumstances in which the judge's discretion should be exercised, should be defined. They found that the existing rule encouraged a rich plaintiff to oppress a poor person with a groundless claim, or gave opportunities for a defendant, often with the resources of an Insurance Company behind him to use obstructive tactics in resisting a just claim by a poor person.

The specification of definite principles had little or no effect in persuading judges to order payment of costs. In one case [2] where damages of £200 were awarded against a co-respondent an order for payment of the costs of the poor person's solicitor was refused, Mr. Justice Bucknill holding that the ability of the co-respondent to pay such costs did not amount to "special circumstances" within the meaning of the rule. This position was naturally galling to conducting solicitors and when the Associated Law Societies of Wales refused to handle any further poor persons' cases one of the reforms they demanded was that the fact that one of the parties was a poor person should have no bearing on the ordinary liability for costs of any other party to the action or suit. The Law Society agreed to consider this proposal and later instructed counsel to draft new rules which go a long way towards meeting the demands of the Welsh Law Societies. They include a provision that "where the means of any party or any other special circumstances of the case justify the making of an order" the opponent should be ordered to pay the "costs of the poor person, including profit costs and

[1] Law Society's Annual Report, 1935.
[2] Jackson *v.* Jackson, 1936, W.N., 266.

fees to counsel, but not court fees, or a proportion of such costs, or a sum of money in respect thereof". The court was to have power to refuse leave to enforce the order if the opponent had not the means to pay.[1] Nothing more has been heard of these draft rules and the position is still that because a man sues, or is sued by, a poor person in the High Court he escapes the usual risk that he will be made liable for his opponent's costs.

It seems clear that this rule, which is found in no other system of legal aid, is based largely on an excessive regard for professional etiquette and legal theory and possibly also on a defective line of reasoning.

It was introduced as a consequence of the opposition of the Bar to the first Draft of the Poor Persons' Rules in 1912. The Bar protested that payment by the opponent, but not by the poor person, was an infringement of the "primary rule of Bar morality" that payment of counsel should not be affected by the result of a case.[2] It is difficult to see what is immoral about the practice, especially as, in this country, barristers have no direct contact with the client and are not interested, therefore, in promoting speculative litigation. The Law Journal evidently did not consider that there was any difficulty in the case of solicitors, for it suggested[3] the solution that only solicitors' charges should be recoverable. Nevertheless, the rule which was finally adopted applied equally to both branches of the profession and, until 1939, the Law Society accepted this as the normal position. The Draft Rules which they have prepared constitute a new departure in that they suggest that an opponent should pay the lawyers' fees if he can. There seems no reason why he should not also be ordered to pay court fees in appropriate circumstances.

The legal theory which stands in the way of making a poor person's opponent liable for costs is that an order for payment of the other party's costs constitutes an indemnity and if the poor person is not liable to pay his own solicitor and counsel and court fees there can be no liability on the part of the opponent. This principle occasionally causes difficulty when a charitable society such as the Bentham Committee or Cambridge House arranges free representation in the County Court. A judge may say, when asked to make an order for payment by the opponent of the poor person's costs, "But under your Society's rules you are

[1] Law Society's Annual Report, 1939.
[2] 47 *L.J.*, 48.
[3] 47 *L.J.*, 48.

not entitled to any fees from your client; that being so there are no costs which I can order your client's unsuccessful opponent to pay, except court fees and out-of-pocket expenses." The point is often ignored, however, for it is obviously unfair that, because the solicitor has accepted the case from a charitable organization, the opponent should escape the costs which in any other circumstances he would have to pay. If costs are paid in these cases they are donated to the funds of the Bentham Committee or Cambridge House and go to help to provide representation in further cases. Under the Manchester scheme they are pocketed by the solicitors and form some compensation for the cases in which they receive no payment.

The other idea which may have had some influence on the development of the existing rule, is that, as the opponent can never receive costs from the poor person (except in a case of misrepresentation or fraud) it is only fair that he should not have to pay costs to the poor person. In practice, of course, this simply benefits the wrong people. It excuses the 97 per cent. of poor persons' opponents who would normally have to pay costs and it does not help the 3 per cent. who would normally have their costs paid; it penalizes conducting solicitors and the Treasury in 97 per cent. of the cases and it does not help them in the remaining 3 per cent.

The absurdity of this position was criticized by Gurney Champion and the *Law Journal* said [1] of his suggestions: "Some of them, as, for example, that where the poor person is successful, the defeated party should be liable for costs, of which part should go to the solicitor and counsel concerned and part to the financing of the scheme, seem to us to be perfectly reasonable and to demand careful consideration." It is not necessary to consider at this stage whether the solicitor and counsel should retain the whole or only part of the costs but it is clear that in any case payment by the opposing party would assist in the running of the scheme.

There is still the liability of the poor person himself to be considered. He can be ordered to pay his own "solicitor and client" costs out of any property which is recovered by the proceedings, subject only to a certain proportion of the amount recovered being left with him. Normally, of course, a successful party has most of his costs paid by his opponent, and if the earlier suggestions made in this chapter were adopted this would be the position in poor persons' cases, except that, in matrimonial

[1] 61 *L.J.*, 319.

cases in particular, there would be a larger proportion of cases in which costs would not, in practice, be recovered, owing to the poverty of the opponent. But in addition to these "party and party" costs there is usually a further bill due to the solicitor, and there will also be some cases where no costs will be paid by the opposing party. There seems no reason why a poor person should not pay any costs for which he would be liable in a normal case if he acquires sufficient means, and whether he acquires these means as a result of the action or otherwise.

It has, moreover, been pointed out [1] that in theory equality before the law demands that a poor person should not be exempted from liability for his opponent's costs simply because he is receiving legal aid. The first thoughts which spring to one's mind at such a proposal are that it would be a hardship to the poor person and that in practice it would make no difference because he would not be able to pay. But as regards the latter it is always possible that a poor person will acquire property before execution of the judgment is barred by the Statutes of Limitation, and in this case there is no reason why he should not indemnify his opponent. As regards the former, Dr. Cohn makes a strong point when he says :

> With the same logic it would be possible to argue that no judgment for the payment of money should be given at all against an assisted defendant. Undue hardships must be prevented by those rules which limit the execution of judgments by withdrawing certain assets from execution : it is not the task of the rules dealing with legal aid or with the relation between poor parties and their opponents in general.

It does seem wrong, however, that a poor man should have his small amount of furniture or savings taken in execution through merely having failed in a case which the certifying authority considered it reasonable for him to bring or defend, and it would appear sound common sense to limit execution by requiring the court to be satisfied that the party in question has sufficient means. In fact this is already done, in connection with the opponent's liability, by the existing Poor Persons' Rules,[2] so the principle that additional safeguards are necessary in these cases has already been recognized. A working basis for the exercise of the court's discretion might be the presumption that a party was only able to pay the same proportion of his opponent's costs as of his own. In this way the liability of a party who was

[1] E. J. Cohn, 59 *L.Q.R.*, 373, 374. [2] Order xvi, rule 31B (5).

receiving partial legal aid would be established unless evidence to the contrary was forthcoming.

Unfortunately, it is clear that, whether the assisted person is theoretically liable to pay his opponent's costs or not, a successful opponent will often not obtain full, or any, satisfaction from this source. It is, therefore, thought by many people that a fund should be provided for the purpose of paying the opponent's costs when they have been awarded by the court and the assisted person has not been able to pay them. It is a difficult question. It may be said that the State has enabled a man of no means to bring an action which he could not otherwise have brought, and has thus indirectly penalized the opponent who, though successful, cannot recover his costs from the assisted person. On the other side is the argument that it is the primary duty of the State to see that its courts are open to all. It has introduced a system of costs which results in the general practice that a successful party to an action is partially reimbursed for the expense to which he has been put by the action. But does the State by fulfilling its primary duty place itself under an obligation to the assisted person's opponent? It is not only in cases where a poor person's certificate has been granted that a party against whom an award of costs has been made cannot, in practice be made to pay them. Is the State to guarantee that in these particular cases, if an order for costs is obtained, they will be paid? There is no precedent for this and no example of the practice in other countries. Nevertheless one cannot escape the conviction that the opponent will have a legitimate grievance unless something is done for him. It is perhaps too much to expect that the State will itself provide a fund out of which costs will be paid to Insurance Companies and local authorities, as well as to people of small means, who have sued, or been sued by, assisted persons, but it might organize some form of compensation fund by a levy on sums recovered in other assisted cases; this is discussed later under general financial proposals. The number of successful opponents would in any event be small though not as small as at present when the great bulk of the cases is composed of undefended divorce petitions and when other actions are usually rejected unless they stand an unwarrantably high chance of success.

CHAPTER X

LEGAL AID IN ALL COURTS

The survey of our own and foreign systems has shown that four things have commonly been considered necessary to enable a poor person to conduct legal proceedings—exemption from court fees, exemption from giving security for costs, representation, and assistance with out-of-pocket expenses. Apart from the last the Poor Persons' Procedure covers all these points but this procedure applies only to the High Court and Court of Appeal, while there are different provisions for the House of Lords and for criminal cases.

The Acts relating to poor prisoners have already been described. In some respects they are superior to the rules for civil cases but they have frequently been criticized, so far as their operation in practice is concerned, on two grounds, first that the remuneration of solicitors and counsel is inadequate for a complicated case, secondly that legal aid is too seldom granted by magistrates.

Some of the severest criticisms are to be found in *English Justice* by " Solicitor ", where a description is given of the conduct of a criminal defence in a case where there is money and in one where there is not.[1] The solution proposed—and this was advanced in a Bill introduced as long ago as 1902—is that the costs of the defence should be paid by the State on the same scale as those of the prosecution. Certainly when one considers the principles of our criminal law that a man is innocent until he is proved guilty, and that it is better than ninety-nine guilty men should go free than that one innocent man should be convicted, it is surprising that the unlimited resources of the State should be brought to the assistance of the prosecution while the defence is stinted.

The reluctance of magistrates to grant legal aid is indisputable having regard to the fact that only 327 legal aid certificates were granted for all the cases tried by magistrates in 1938.[2] Many Police Court cases are, of course, trivial, but many are not. In the year 1938, 19,079 people were sent to prison by these

[1] Pp. 157–60 in the Pelican Edition.

[2] Statistical Abstract for the British Empire, 1939. Cmd. 6140, p. 184. During the war considerably less have been granted.

courts without the option of a fine [1] and, as the Finlay Committee pointed out,[2] the consequences of a conviction, particularly of first offenders, may be extremely serious. " Solicitor ", whose experience of Police Courts is obviously extensive, states that miscarriages of justice undoubtedly arise and that legal aid is doubly necessary owing to the fact that magistrates are often untrained, while the speed with which cases are heard in the police court and the tendencies in some courts to rush the prisoner into summary trial and to refuse bail, add to the prisoner's difficulties.[3]

In America the Public Defender, or, as he is called when not employed by the State, Private Defender, is popular with the Legal Aid Associations. It is said that assigned counsel are liable to be young and inexperienced or else older men who are not able to get work through the usual channels and that the Defender system makes for efficiency and responsibility, and is probably twice as cheap.[4] As has been noted, the Scottish Committee has recommended that a Public Defensor should be appointed for the Police Courts in Scotland [5] although the Finlay Committee considered that, amongst other objections, there were insufficient cases to justify such an appointment in England.[6]

Whether or not the Defender system is desirable in this country there appears to be little demand for the change. It might, however, be advantageous, both from the point of view of expense and of finding out more about the working of the Acts, to bring the criminal provisions under the same control as legal aid in civil matters. It can only be confusing and wasteful to have two different sets of machinery for carrying out the same functions.

The rules applying to the House of Lords were described in Chapter IV. In themselves they are inadequate, for it is difficult to see how a pauper can himself find the out-of-pocket expenses of his appeal, including the cost of forty copies of the Appellant's and Respondent's " Cases ", twenty-five of them printed, and numerous copies of other documents, which have to be lodged.[7] Moreover no professional assistance is provided for arguing a case before the Lords of Appeal but this astonishing omission

[1] Home Office Criminal Statistics; Cmd. 6167.
[2] Cmd. 2638, para. 15.
[3] *English Justice*, Chapter II.
[4] R. Heber Smith and Bradway: *Growth of Legal Aid Work in the U.S.A.* Department of Labor Bulletin, No. 607, 1936, Chapter XI.
[5] Cmd. 5435, para. 59. [6] Cmd. 2638, para. 21.
[7] House of Lords: Method of Procedure and Standing Orders, Direction 32.

is doubtless due to the fact that, in normal times at least, solicitors and counsel can always be found who are willing to act free in such cases, either out of professional interest in an important case or for the reputation which they will earn for acting in an appeal to the House of Lords. The legal profession can be relied on to see that where leave to sue *in forma pauperis* has been granted the question of their fees will not prevent the appeal going ahead, although they can hardly be expected to pay the disbursements, but when a would-be Appellant has just too much money to qualify for the *in forma pauperis* procedure the position is hopeless. Not only are the fees of the House and of his lawyers payable but he is required to find security for £700, in all,[1] which gives some indication of the amount of the costs which each of the parties is likely to incur in the appeal. It has seemed to many writers that if a case merits an appeal from the Court of Appeal the point at issue is of sufficient public concern to warrant a decision from the House of Lords at the public expense irrespective of the poverty of the parties. If that view is not accepted, then further measures of legal aid are needed. However, it is a very small number of people who are unlucky enough to be martyred at the block of the English system of "precedents" and the courts where the absence of legal aid causes real hardship are the County Courts and, in civil cases, the Police Courts.

It has been estimated * that the Poor Persons' Procedure (in 1928) covered only 2¼ per cent. of the needs of the poor and that of the remainder 10 per cent. were quasi-civil cases in the Police Courts and 62⅝ per cent. County Court cases. The figures may be questioned, but there can be no doubt that in the two courts where the poor most frequently require to bring civil proceedings no legal aid is provided, except that in the Police Courts the magistrates have power to remit fees. The position in the two courts may be considered together, for the same points apply to each. The Police Court deals with separation and maintenance cases, with affiliation, and also with claims for the recovery of possession of houses of a low rental and with certain claims between master and servant ; the County

[1] Standing Order 5.

* According to Mr. Harrington Edwards in a paper read to the Law Society on 6th October, 1928. The other figures given are :

2 per cent. divorce cases.
¼ per cent. other High Court cases taken by the Poor Persons' Department.
⅛ per cent. High Court cases not taken by the Poor Persons' Department.
25 per cent. criminal cases.

Court deals with practically all classes of civil actions where the amount involved is not very high.

Criticism of the absence of legal aid in the County Court was made by the Court of Appeal in Cook *v.* Imperial Tobacco Company,[1] where Younger L. J. said there was a grave risk of miscarriage of justice and Atkin L. J. said " there is no power of proceeding *in forma pauperis* in the County Court and a poor person without any means may lose all legal redress ". The actual point involved in that decision, namely that a person who had been granted legal aid in the High Court might be ordered to provide security for costs or else have his proceedings transferred to the County Court, where there was no legal aid, was recognized by the Finlay Committee as an anomaly [2] and legal aid in the County Court was introduced for this special case. It might be said, however, that it is just as much of an anomaly that a case which has been started in the High Court should receive legal aid, while a similar case started in the County Court can get none.

It would appear hardly necessary to argue that there should be power to remit court fees in the County Court when a poor person has reasonable grounds for action. Such remission is allowed in the Police Court, where the fees are very much smaller but, except in Workmen's Compensation cases, fees always have to be paid in the County Court and although a County Court action is usually considerably cheaper than a similar High Court action, the fees for a summons are sometimes more than for a writ. Unfortunately the proposal that there should be power to remit County Court fees, a proposal supported by the Council of County Court Judges, was rejected by the Finlay Committee on the ground that it would encourage litigation.[3] The Committee did " not think poverty prevents the litigation of any appreciable number of claims of real merit ".[4] " Yet," as Mr. Mervyn Jones says, " it is difficult to see how, without money, any claim can be litigated at all. The County Court is pre-eminently the poor man's court. But no claim can be brought before it—even in person—until court fees are paid. Yet more fees must be paid before the plaintiff can be heard. No money, no justice." [5] Yet more fees, it might be added, have to be paid before a judgment can be enforced, as is frequently neces-

[1] 1922, 2 *K.B.*, 158.
[2] Cmd. 3016, para. 15. [3] Para. 14. [4] Para. 20.
[5] J. Mervyn Jones : *Free Legal Advice in England and Wales* (1940), p. 54.

sary in contested actions in these Courts. So far as encouraging litigation is concerned it is the opinion of Mr. Mervyn Jones that the absence of legal aid in County Courts accounts, in part, for the continued existence of "ambulance-chasing agencies", and of Dr. Jackson that it encourages many unjustified actions which are only brought because they probably will not be contested. Dr. Cohn endorses both opinions.[1]

The Committee also rejected all proposals involving representation in the County Courts. The extension of the Poor Persons' Rules would be too onerous, legal aid as a benefit under the National Health Acts was "unworkable"; Legal Dispensaries or Hospitals were undesirable because "it is manifestly in the interests of a State that its citizens should be healthy, not that they should be litigious"; a State or municipal scheme was "destructive of the relationship of solicitor and client", would give rise to "grave difficulties" and the weight of evidence was strongly against it; and a subsidy for Poor Man's Lawyers was unnecessary and would involve supervision, which would be unpopular.[2] A minority report by two of the members of the Committee recommended that advice should be provided by salaried legal advisers employed by the local authorities and that the Poor Persons' Rules should be extended to the County Courts and Police Courts.

Approaching this question of representation from the basis that the poor man should have a reasonably equal chance of prosecuting his case against a wealthier opponent, two questions may be asked—"Is representation needed in these courts?" and "Can the poor man obtain it?"

Let us grant straight away that there are County Court cases where representation is not needed. Summonses can be issued without any other assistance than that of the Clerks, or a Poor Man's Lawyer if one is available. Many cases are settled without a hearing and a man who is reasonably intelligent and who has had previous experience, or instructions how to proceed, can conduct a simple debt-collecting case without a lawyer.

On the other hand there can be no doubt whatever that there are many cases where a lawyer is essential.

Small claims can be just as difficult, as regards both law and evidence, as large ones,* and in any case the County Court

[1] E. J. Cohn: 59 *L.Q.R.*, 269. [2] Cmd. 3016, paras. 13 and 16–19.

* This is recognized by the fact that, however small the value of the subject-matter, the County Court may certify that the case is "fit for counsel".

can no longer be regarded as a Small Claims Court; in 1850 the £20 limit to claims which might be brought there was raised to £50, in 1903 to £100 and in 1938 to £200. Moreover, new matters of great complexity have been added. In the face of the findings of the Finlay Committee, which had then recently been published, the *Solicitors' Journal* stated [1]: "The County Courts, although originally conceived as courts for the recovery of small debts, deal with matters of great importance and complexity, and the time has come when this should be recognized, and the poor litigant receive the aid without which his right to resort to the courts is an empty one," and Sir Edward Parry, a County Court Judge for thirty-three years, wrote [2]:

> There is considerable evidence in the wording of the report that the Committee did not understand the real nature of the problem before them. "It must be remembered," they write, "that a large proportion of the cases in the County Court are simple in character and the Judge is well able to ascertain the facts, so that it is neither necessary nor advantageous that there should be any legal assistance at all." Why must that be remembered which has no foundation in fact? Who told the Committee that County Court cases were simple? And why were they so simple as to believe it? If their conclusion is sound and legal assistance is "neither necessary nor advantageous", why not abolish it altogether? It is a revolutionary proposition, no doubt, but it has had considerable support ever since Jack Cade raised his standard on Blackheath and Dick, his henchman, moved the resolution: "The first thing we do, let's kill all the lawyers." I agree with the Committee to this extent, that if lawyers are not necessary neither side should have them, but if they are necessary, both sides should be equally equipped.
>
> And the suggestion that all a County Court Judge has to do in his day's work is to unravel a few simple facts, that he has no legal problems to trouble him, and that his work is intellectually of a lower order than that of the High Court Judge, is another misconception of the obvious. A judge of a County Court has a far wider range of civil law to master than any other judicial functionary in the Kingdom. Take as two examples of the sweet simplicity of legal matters in the County Court, which no High Court Judge is entrusted with, the Workmen's Compensation Act and the Rent Restriction Acts . . .

Complicated law may equally be involved in the "quasi civil" cases dealt with in the Police Court: points may arise with regard to Rent Restrictions, wages disputes and affiliation and matrimonial cases which require a thorough knowledge of the relevant Acts and precedents. The Finlay Committee did in fact recommend, in its first report, that legal aid should be

[1] 72 *S.J.*, 310. [2] *The Gospel and the Law.*

available in bastardy and maintenance cases,[1] but the recommendation was not carried out. Admittedly the magistrate may not be a lawyer himself but one might say, as *Solicitor* does,[2] that this fact gives an even greater advantage to the party who is represented by a lawyer. And it is not only a question of law: training is necessary to elucidate and marshal the facts of a case. To prove the ownership of goods which are claimed by both the parties requires a systematic building up of all the facts which can help one's case, dexterity in presenting them and in cross-examining the opposing party and his witnesses. Proof of adultery is sometimes so technical and involves such serious issues that a County Court Judge is still not considered fit to try even undefended cases of divorce, yet this question is expected to be fought out in the Police Court by working-class wives and husbands in cases which may result in separation and the burden of a weekly payment for an indefinite period.*

At the meeting called by the London Council of Social Service after the second report of the Finlay Committee, Mr. William Latey pointed out that the few appeals from the magistrates which succeeded in reaching the Divisional Court showed how necessary legal aid in Police Court matrimonial cases was and the late Sir John Withers, M.P., disclosed the fact that he had tried to convince the Committee of the need for remission of fees and representation in both the County Courts and Police Courts.[3]

Denial of the need for representation comes from a surprising source when Mr. Claud Mullins is found taking up this position. It is entirely inconsistent with certain preceding comments in his book *In Quest of Justice* where he demonstrates the enormous cost of some County Court cases, agrees with Sir Edward Parry as to the legal difficulties of County Court cases and remarks that the number of litigants who appear in person adds considerably to the judge's responsibilities and difficulties. But Mr. Mullins is impressed by the desirability of dealing with this problem by conciliation rather than litigation, and it is perhaps that which leads him to make the remark: "My own experience leads me to believe that, apart from giving legal advice, no

[1] Cmd. 2638, para. 17.

[2] *English Justice*, pp. 49–51, in the Pelican Edition.

* The order may also be treated by the Divorce Court as sufficient proof of adultery, desertion, or other ground on which it was granted, and a divorce decree may be pronounced after evidence has been given by the Petitioner only.

[3] 165 *L.T.*, 402.

assistance should be necessary for the conduct of poor persons' cases in the minor courts, *thanks to the almost bottomless fund of sympathy and patience possessed by the average County Court Judge.*" [1]

Every Poor Man's Lawyer will wish to add his tribute to the quality of the County Court Judge, a quality so greatly described by Francis Bacon: "A judge ought to prepare his way to a just sentence, as God useth to prepare his way, by raising valleys and taking down hills, so that when there appeareth on either side an high hand, violent prosecution, cunning advantages taken, combination, great power, great counsel, then is the virtue of a judge seen, to make inequality equal, that he may plant his judgment as upon an even ground." But the suggestion that the virtue of the judge can make representation unnecessary was exploded over a hundred years ago in an article in the *Edinburgh Review*, attributed to Sydney Smith. The article was written against the practice then in force of not allowing counsel to prisoners accused of felony, but if the necessary terms are transposed the points which the passage makes are as relevant to civil cases to-day as they were to criminal cases in 1826.[2]

> Of all false and foolish dicta, the most trite and the most absurd, is that which asserts that the Judge is counsel for the prisoner. We do not hesitate to say that this is merely an unmeaning phrase, invented to defend a pernicious abuse. The Judge *cannot* be counsel for the prisoner, *ought not* to be counsel for the prisoner, never *is* counsel for the prisoner. To force an ignorant man into a court of justice, and to tell him that the Judge is his counsel appears to us quite as foolish, as to set an hungry man down to his meals, and to tell him that the table was his dinner. In the first place a counsel should always have private and previous communication with the prisoner, which the Judge, of course, cannot have. The prisoner reveals to his counsel how far he is guilty, or he is not; states to him all the circumstances of his case—and might often enable his advocate, if his advocate were allowed to speak, to explain a long string of circumstantial evidence, in a manner favourable to the innocence of his client. Of all these advantages, the Judge, if he had every disposition to befriend the prisoner, is of course deprived. Something occurs to the prisoner in the course of the cause; he suggests it in a whisper to his counsel, doubtful if it is a wise point to urge or not. His counsel thinks it of importance, and would urge it, if his mouth were not shut. Can a prisoner have this secret communication with a Judge, and take his advice, whether or not he, the Judge, shall mention it to the Jury? . . . He (counsel) is brought there (or would be brought there if the privilege of speech were allowed) for the express purpose of saying all that could be said on one side of the question. He is a weight in *one* scale and someone else holds the

[1] Chap. XIX. [2] *Edinburgh Review*, 1826: "*Counsel for Prisoners.*"

balance. This is the way in which truth is elicited in civil, and would be in criminal cases. . . .

In fact the only meaning of the phrase is this, that the Judge will not suffer any undue advantage to be taken of the ignorance and helplessness of the prisoner—that he will point out any evidence or circumstance in his favour—and see that equal justice is done to both parties. But in this sense he is as much the counsel of the prosecutor as of the prisoner. This is all the Judge can do, or even pretends to do ; but he can have no previous communication with the prisoner—he can have no confidential communication in court with the prisoner before he sums up ; he cannot fling the whole weight of his understanding into the opposite scale against the counsel for the prosecution, and produce that collision of faculties, which, in all other cases but those of felony, is supposed to be the happiest method of arriving at truth.

Is there any one gentleman in the House of Commons, who, in yielding his vote to this paltry and perilous fallacy of the Judge being counsel for the prisoner, does not feel, that, were he himself a criminal, he would prefer almost any counsel, at the bar, to the tender mercies of the Judge? How strange that any man who could make his election would eagerly and diligently surrender this exquisite privilege, and addict himself to the perilous practice of giving fees to counsel.

The writer goes on to describe the situation of a poor man appearing in court on his own behalf:

Can a sick man find strength and nerves to speak before a large assembly?—can an ignorant man find words?—can a low man find confidence? Is he not afraid of becoming an object of ridicule?—can he believe that his expressions will be understood? How often have we seen a poor wretch, struggling against the agonies of his spirit, and the rudeness of his conceptions, and his awe of better dressed men and better taught men . . .

The folly of being counsel for yourself is so notorious in civil cases, that it is grown into a proverb.

It is only necessary to add that among the working classes, and particularly women, there is a deep-rooted horror of having to speak for themselves in court. The idea of appearing in court suggests to them some disgrace, associated, no doubt, with being prosecuted or with having to disclose intimate domestic troubles, but applying also to the County Court. Every Poor Man's lawyer is familiar with the embarrassment and shake of the head which greets the advice to issue a Summons personally—"I never have been in one of them places" or "When I tried to do it once before I couldn't get a word out". Even a professional advocate, remembering his first few appearances in court, will sympathize with this last remark. In practice the working class man or woman will often drop a case rather than conduct it personally and of the loss which results from this there is the tangible proof that a Poor Man's Lawyer, or, indeed, any other lawyer, is regularly consulted by people who have received offers from Insurance Companies or others to settle their claims for a few pounds, and, as soon as it is known that a solicitor is acting, the offer is increased enormously and possibly is increased still further if a Summons is issued. The advantage of professional assistance is not confined to actions for damages. As Mr. Harrington Edwards said in a paper read to the Law Society in 1928,[1] if matters are so simple as has been made out, neither side should have counsel or solicitor—" it is not to be expected that the Law Society or the Bar Council would ever welcome such a proposal ; if it were seriously suggested it is believed that nothing more would be heard of the 'simplicity' of the cases in the County Court ".

The other question which remains is whether a poor person is in fact able to obtain representation in the County and Police Courts when he needs it. In some cases he is. If, for example, he is a member of a Trade Union he is very likely to be able to obtain excellent professional assistance in a workman's accident case, and a member of an Approved Society may be assisted up to a point, but in any other circumstances he is dependent on charity, which may or may not be available, or he must pay a solicitor's, and possibly counsel's, fees in the usual way.

As far as charity is concerned there are one or two societies which deal with specific matters, such as the Women's and Children's Protection Society and then there are the organizations for assisting poor litigants in general.

There are only two well-established schemes which provide representation without the solicitor receiving any payment, even if successful. At Cambridge House two or three cases a month are taken up on this basis. Cases are only referred to honorary solicitors when the centre cannot itself obtain a settlement or when there is special difficulty, and even then applications are excluded on various grounds, for example, where there is not likely to be a judgment which will be of much value to the applicant, and where the applicant could take proceedings personally or could probably get a solicitor to conduct the case for him on a semi-speculative basis. In only ten cases a year at most are proceedings taken by solicitors who do not expect remuneration

[1] *The Poor and the Law in 1928*; 166 *L.T.*, pp. 233 ff.

in any event, although there are many more which would be included if the facilities were sufficient. The Bentham Committee, the other completely charitable scheme, arranged for free representation in 52 successful, and 16 unsuccessful, cases in 1938–9 and in 18 successful, and 10 unsuccessful, cases in 1939–40. Even before the war there was a shortage of solicitors and the fact that the number of cases in which there have been settlements or successful proceedings has now dropped to one-quarter of the pre-war figure shows on what unreliable ground the system rests.* The Bentham Committee has itself recommended that a system of payment for representation should be adopted.[1]

Undoubtedly the majority of cases find their way into the hands of speculative solicitors. This is what Sir Edward Parry said about it: [2]

> The poor cannot bring their compensation cases or running down cases into court themselves, and, as the (Finlay) Committee points out, they go to well advertised societies which are " merely devices used by solicitors of a speculative type to obtain work ". It is admitted that the voluntary societies are not equal to the demand and I hold no brief for the speculative solicitor. It has been my task on occasion to check his rapacity. But it is cant to deplore his activities when we can only fold our hands and do nothing effective ourselves to help the poor.

It would be an abuse of the popular meaning of the word to call the system run by the Birmingham Poor Man's Lawyer Association " speculative " but under the Rules the solicitors who take up cases can only receive payment if they succeed in getting an award of costs from the opposing party. It is acknowledged that this system is really only effective in Workmen's Compensation cases and there is a technical flaw in it which was raised in the course of the discussion on costs.

To avoid the professional objections to this practice and also because it is to some extent more equitable and the only way, even in normal times, that anything like an adequate number of conducting solicitors can be found, the Manchester and Salford Poor Man's Lawyer Association allows the solicitors to charge the client fees, on the understanding that his means will be taken into account, and this is the system followed by most of the Poor Man's Lawyers that provide representation at all.

* The figures are: 1938–9, settled 236, successful proceedings, 52; 1942–3, settled cases and successful proceedings, 72.

[1] In a Memorandum addressed to the Secretary of the Law Society in 1943 and in evidence submitted to the Rushcliffe Committee, 1944.

[2] *The Gospel and the Law.*

No doubt supervision by a highly professional body prevents the worst abuses to which such a system lends itself, but it is inevitable that some solicitors, when they know that their client's pocket is not deep enough to pay them an adequate fee, will be reluctant to take proceedings unless the case is a practically certain winner, or will settle for a smaller sum than they would have demanded if there had been funds to fight the case to a conclusion. Again, a strong accident claim stands a good chance of being taken up, but where is the solicitor who is going to act free in cases where the decision is doubtful, or where the opponent is a poor man as well as the client, or where the claim is not for damages and there is little prospect of either side paying for the work that is done?

In fact a solicitor could not afford to make a practice of risking the costs which are involved in some of these cases. Consider the figures for the cost of County Court cases quoted by Mr. Mullins [1] and supplied to him by the Registrar of a London Court. These are, no doubt, glaring examples of high costs, but on the other hand some of them will have been taxed by the court on a party and party basis so that normally the solicitor would have a claim for further fees against his own client:

	Nature of Claim	Amount Claimed £ s. d.	Amount of Judgment £ s. d.	Scale	Amount of Taxed Costs £ s. d.	Remarks
1.	Money lent	100	100	C	55 11 6	Defendant did not appear
2.	Damages for negligence	16 19 4	12 8 4	A	13 14 2	
3.	"	30	Defendant won	B	30 7 4	
4.	"	22	22	C	47 10 5	The Judge made a special order that costs should be on a higher scale.
5.	Possession of House		Possession	B	22 7 6	
6.	Possession and rent	100	Possession and £100	C	44 10 3	
7.	Rent	16 13 4	16 13 4	A	10 8 8	
8.	School fees	9 9 0	9 9 0	Lower	4 2 6	Certificate for Counsel.
9.	Dishonoured cheque	20	20	A	10 8 5	
10.	Damages for negligence	56	Defendant won	C	28 3 9	
11.	Work done	40 17 3	25	B	24 14 4	
12.	Detention of goods	27 7 1	Defendant won	B	35 4 6	

[1] *In Quest of Justice.*

Can a poor man or a poor man's solicitor afford to run up such bills in the hope that the opposing party will pay them?

Even if the solicitor is prepared to give his own time and services free there will probably be considerable expenses with which he will have to assist if the case is to continue. The following figures are given by *A Barrister* [1] as the cost to a workman of a normal Workman's Compensation case, excluding the costs of his solicitor:

	£	*s.*	*d.*
Medical Report	2	2	0
Counsel's opinion	2	4	6
Advice on Evidence	2	4	6
General practitioner as witness	2	2	0
Counsel's brief	6	16	0
Conduct money for, say, 2 witnesses	1	0	0
	£16	9	0

Counsel's Opinion and Advice might be dispensed with; on the other hand it might be necessary to have a specialist to give medical evidence, at a cost of at least 10 guineas, and to have a Request for a Medical Referee as Assessor, costing a further 3 guineas, or expert evidence as to machinery or some other matter. In cases other than Workmen's Compensation cases court fees have to be paid in addition.

In poor districts solicitors are particularly hard to get for these cases. Thus in Poplar the Citizens' Advice Bureau pays fees to a solicitor for representing applicants in minor cases which are not considered worth the trouble and delay of referring to the Bentham Committee. In this way local people have successfully opposed several claims for rent or possession of a house which otherwise would probably have been decided against the poor person, and judgments or settlements have been obtained in such claims as wrongful detention of property, arrears on separation deeds, sale of worthless goods and lost laundry. Toynbee Hall used to pay an annual retaining fee to a solicitor before the present war but this has lapsed and few other charitable organizations have been in a position to meet this expense.

But even if the Poor Man's Lawyer Associations did provide adequate assistance in the County Courts and Police Courts, a claim which few, if any, of them would make, there are still large areas of the country where no such arrangements exist.

[1] "A Barrister": *Justice in England*, 1938.

The Bentham Committee's small resources extend only to the administrative County of London and Citizens' Advice Bureaux in outer London experience great difficulty in obtaining representation. In towns of the size of Blackburn, Bolton, Bristol, Cardiff, Coventry, any assistance which may be given depends on the view which a particular solicitor takes of his charitable obligations ; a glance at the list of towns of over 100,000 population in the Appendix will show how little organization exists in the provinces for court proceedings. Where a number of lawyers have joined together in a philanthropic scheme which is conscientiously conducted, the would-be litigant stands a better chance, but even these schemes have their ups and downs. In the smaller towns the attitude usually is that there is no need for a scheme since solicitors are always ready to help deserving cases. Perhaps they are, but it requires little imagination to put oneself in the shoes of a poor man entering an entirely unknown solicitor's office and saying " I have no money but I want you to fight this case for me out of charity ". As was said in a leading article in *The Times* in 1912,[1] " It is mockery to tell persons friendless and unknown to go to a solicitor and inform him of the wrong." Even where there is not this difficulty, for example, in cases referred under the Army legal advice scheme, which solicitors are more than usually anxious to assist, it has been said by one who takes part in the scheme " As far as aid in litigation is concerned the practice of the Army's legal aid scheme has tended to demonstrate again that the present state of our law fails to provide for all needs." [2]

The Law Society gave evidence to the Finlay Committee that neither remission of fees nor representation was needed in the lower courts except in cases remitted from the High Court to the County Court, and that evidence, at a time when the success of the Poor Person's Procedure of the High Court hung in the balance, no doubt carried a great deal of weight with the Committee. Since then the evidence to the contrary has become even clearer and the Law Society's own report for 1935 contains the passage, " Each year the reports from the various centres indicate that the committees are being appealed to more in respect of such matters as Police Court and County Court proceedings and are giving advice in such matters, although they are not within the ambit of the rules." Yet there are still many lawyers who deny the need for the obvious reforms

[1] 30th December, 1912. [2] E. J. Cohn, 59 *L.Q.R.*, 25.

and one may well ask why it is that solicitors and barristers, who ought to be the first to urge the need for professional assistance and who do regularly express their concern at the increasing number of administrative tribunals before which no representation is allowed, oppose the idea of representation for poor persons?

It is undoubtedly because they are afraid that any scheme would be on the lines of the Poor Person's Procedure in the High Court. Consider this quotation from a lengthy article in the Law Journal in 1925:[1]

> . . . there is no doubt but that the court fees in County Courts are in many cases a severe burden on the poor litigant . . . As to gratuitous assistance, a considerable number of solicitors, more especially in the country, make a very large proportion of their professional livelihood as advocates in County Court cases, and any system by which such services were expected to be performed gratuitously would necessarily press very hardly on those who practise to any considerable extent in County Courts.

It is right that professional organizations and journals should see that members of the profession are not unfairly treated, but the risk of a burden being imposed on lawyers is a reason for proposing a scheme that would work fairly, not for resisting the idea of any scheme at all.

The article continues with regard to Police Courts: "The difficulties of devising any satisfactory scheme seem to be almost insuperable. With regard to Police Courts throughout the country, there is, as in County Courts, a body of solicitors who make their living as advocates in such courts, and it is difficult to conceive a scheme, which would not gravely affect them."

To-day it would be generally agreed that the first thing to look at is the needs of the public as a whole and that the interest of a profession must come second. It will later be suggested, however, that in this case there is no serious, not to mention "insuperable", difficulty in reconciling the two. The 1941 Report of the Standing Committee on Legal Aid Work of the American Bar Association included this sentence: "It cannot be too often stated that the efforts of individual lawyers are inadequate to bring equal justice to all and that organized legal aid steals no paying clients from members of the bar."

As we have seen it is due to historical reasons that the County Court has no provision for legal aid, the Committee which decided against the introduction of a system was lacking in experience

[1] 60 *L.J.*, 213 ff., 237 ff., 261 ff.

of the courts with which it was concerned and it reported at a time of dire national economies. Writing before the war Mr. Mervyn Jones suggested that the Committee " might, in the light of changed conditions, be disposed to reconsider its conclusions ", and Lord Maugham wrote that the Report was " to a large extent out-of-date ".[1] Since then it has been described as " more than ever inadequate and out-of-date "[2] and its Report as belonging " to a period whose views and methods belong to the past—and irredeemably so ".[3]

As a possible alternative to legal aid in the inferior courts some consideration ought to be given to the system of Small Claims Courts and Domestic Relations Courts which is found in many States of America. A typical Small Claims Court is described in *Legal Aid Work in the U.S.A.* There is an entrance fee of $1 or $2. The plaintiff states his case to a clerk, who enters a simple statement of claim in a book, which the plaintiff signs. The clerk sends a notice by registered post to the defendant, requiring him to state his defence by a certain date and to appear before the court on a certain date. The judge obtains the evidence by putting questions to the parties and their witnesses, not necessarily following strictly the rules of evidence. Cases can be heard within ten days of the claim being made. Appeals are allowed in some States but not in others; sometimes they are allowed only on the ground that substantial justice has not been done; a fee is payable by the appellant and appeals are not numerous. The claims which can be brought in these courts vary from $20 to $200 and only about 25 per cent. of the claims are contested. Speed and cheapness are the aims of the Small Claims Courts and where these are more needed than thoroughness the procedure has much to commend it. It has, however, been criticized by Gurney Champion[4] as making for a multiplicity of different courts, and by Dr. Cohn,[5] who points out that the law may be just as difficult when there is a small amount at stake as when the amount is large and that a relatively small sum may be very important to a poor plaintiff. Altogether there is little enthusiasm for such courts in this country, although some of the lessons which they teach might be incorporated in the practice of our County Courts.

[1] J. Mervyn Jones: op. cit., pp. 4 and 54.
[2] Bentham Committee's Memorandum to the Law Society, 1943.
[3] E. J. Cohn, 59 *L.Q.R.*, 250.
[4] F. C. G. Gurney Champion: *Justice and the Poor in England* (1926).
[5] E. J. Cohn, 59 *L.Q.R.*, 269.

There are few people with experience of poor persons' cases who would now deny that there is a need for power to remit court fees in the County Court, as well as in the Police Court and that in both Courts there is need for representation in some cases.

For the sake of completeness it should be added that representation should also be provided for some of the matters which come before administrative tribunals. There is a tendency to prohibit legal representation before such tribunals, as has been done, for example, in the case of Hardship Tribunals held under the Military Service (Armed Forces) Act. It is not proposed to enter into the controversial question of whether this is a good or a bad tendency but the principle is clear that, if legal representation is permitted at all, it should not be available only to those who can afford the professional fees.

The provision of legal aid in all courts would inevitably entail a certain amount of expense but, if the proposals as to costs which are discussed later were adopted, the amount need not be as large as might appear from studying the accounts of a charitable organization such as the Bentham Committee.* One simply has to accept the fact that if there are many comparatively poor people in the population it is impossible to make justice available to all and at the same time to make justice pay for itself.† The courts do not benefit only those few people who actually need to commence litigation and, in the terms of the conclusion which was adopted unanimously by the judges of the Cleveland Municipal Court [1]—" Believing that Courts as governmental agencies are operated as a part of our social system for the benefit of all, we are unwilling to subscribe to the view that the litigant should pay all the expenses of maintaining the Court."

* Not that the cost of the Bentham Committee (£600 for 1942–3) is particularly high, but it would seem high in relation to the amount of work now being done if it were assumed that most of the work was being done free of charge. In actual fact a large part of the work is done by the part-time salaried secretary.

† This point is discussed in Chapter XIII at p. 129.

[1] Quoted by R. H. Smith : *Justice and the Poor*, Chapter V.

CHAPTER XI

LEGAL ADVICE CENTRES

People who want the poor to have better facilities for bringing legal proceedings are sometimes accused of wanting to encourage litigation. This is far from being the case; practically every writer who deals with this subject stresses the importance of avoiding litigation whenever possible, but the way to do this is not to make the courts inaccessible to all but a small section of the community, but to provide means for advice and conciliation as well as court proceedings.

Litigation must always be a heavy expense to somebody, whether it be the Poor Person, his opponent, the State, or all three. Moreover, a litigious state of mind is not a desirable thing. "Agree with thine adversary whilst thou art in the way" is always the ideal, and litigation is only justifiable when the opponent refuses to make a reasonable settlement or when there is some issue at stake which only a court can decide. It is one of the great defects of the Poor Persons' Rules that they make no provision for legal advice. In practice a great many of the Honorary Secretaries of Poor Persons' Committees feel obliged to give legal advice to applicants, since otherwise unnecessary and needless applications come before the committees or applicants who probably have good claims are unable to prove even a *prima facie* case through ignorance of what evidence is required or means to obtain it.

Cases where litigation is necessary are extremely rare compared with the consultations which are needed for advice, and the number of proceedings taken decreases when advice and assistance out of court are available. There are undoubtedly cases which at present are only prevented from going to court by lack of means and if this disability were removed there would be some increase in litigation but it need not be large. From a more personal point of view the benefit of legal advice to people in distress and difficulty is out of all proportion to the expense and trouble involved and it is noticeable what an effect a few minutes' sympathetic audience can have on the unlearned man's conception of the law. If people to whom the law has always appeared an inaccessible, abstruse and somewhat shady institution find that it really does exist for their guidance and help, their attitude to their democratic rights and duties visibly improves. As John S. Bradway, Director of the Legal Aid Clinic at Duke University, U.S.A., has put it [1]:

> If their visit means nothing more than a desire to find out what the law is, it represents a definite advance towards a desirable reliance by the individual upon legal processes as a method of solving his difficulties. His alternatives are to employ extra-legal, and sometimes illegal, means, or to do nothing, which often results in an undesirable state of mind.

The last point was confirmed by the Finlay Committee [2]:

> We doubt not that frequently the result of the advice given is to show that what has been felt as a grievance is not really a grievance at all. Where there is ignorance of the legal position there is apt to be matured a sense of misfortune and of injustice and it is work of the highest value to the community to remove that sense of grievance and of injustice, where it is unfounded, by the giving of sound legal advice.

But if legal advice is to succeed in its objects it must be good and it must be thorough. It is a mere makeshift to have legal advice given, as most legal advice is now being given, by people who are not trained lawyers. The system used by most of the smaller Citizens' Advice Bureaux, of telephoning the problem to a solicitor and passing on his advice to the enquirer is very little better; it may be adequate for some more or less factual enquiries but for nothing more. A recent example disclosed the fact that social workers considered they were safe in advising that any tenant of furnished premises who had received notice to quit must give up possession. In the particular case a busy solicitor, consulted over the telephone, substantially agreed that this advice might be given, but when the landlord was sued for having ejected the tenant it was found that the notice given was not in order and even if this had not been so there were certain technical points, such as the effect of subsequent correspondence and the Courts (Emergency Powers) Act which had to be considered. It is difficult to convince the average adviser at a Citizens' Advice Bureau or elsewhere that an apparently simple point may need very careful consideration and that it is not safe merely to repeat the same advice as a solicitor has been heard to give in other similar cases. Lawyers are right to insist that a legal training is essential for legal work and foolish to encourage

[1] *Legal Aid Work in the United States*; 24 *Jo. of Comp. Leg.*, 1942, pp. 49 ff.
[2] Cmd. 3016, para. 8.

a state of affairs where untrained people are forced to try to do the lawyer's job for him.

At the "Poor Man's Lawyers" themselves there is usually a rule that only solicitors or barristers or clerks working under supervision shall advise, but this alone is not sufficient to ensure that good advice is given. Most of the advisers in normal times are young solicitors or barristers who come with a genuine desire to help the poor but also to gain experience. There is nothing shameful in the latter motive, but it does mean that they are probably quite unfamiliar with life in a poor district and come from a background which favours landlords and employers and business interests. There is no test of suitability; all offers of help must be gratefully accepted and the applicant must consider himself lucky to be able to see a lawyer of any kind. It is very desirable that anyone who sets himself up as a Poor Man's Lawyer should know and sympathize with the difficulties of the people he is advising, should be thoroughly acquainted with allied social services, both statutory and voluntary, and should not only have the Rent Restriction and Workmen's Compensation Acts at his fingertips but should know how to make himself understood to his enquirer. These qualities take some time to acquire at the rate of one-night-a-week, and, unfortunately, the enthusiasm with which the volunteer starts out on the job frequently wanes when the novelty has worn off. It is not exactly agreeable to make your way to the dirtiest part of the town after a full day's work at the office and to spend the evening listening to the sad and sordid stories of a slum quarter, trying to give advice on unfamiliar topics, often without any books to consult or the time to consult the few that are available, working at high pressure and sometimes astonished at the ingratitude and unpleasantness of those to whom the hoped-for answer cannot be given, though appreciation and commiseration, too, are sometimes shown.

"Do you get paid for doing this?" said one applicant to a Poor Man's Lawyer.

"No."

"Do you do it because you're standing for Parliament?"

"No."

"Then what *do* you do it for?"

Those exceptionally worthy men who do not give up the work just when they have acquired the experience to make them valuable will probably hang on when their minds have become closed to all branches of the law except those few on which they specialize in private practice, perhaps after they have ceased to practise, not realizing the limitations with which time has handicapped them.

But even when the Advisers are sound there are few Poor Man's Lawyers Centres which refute Gurney Champion's condemnation of the system as " legal haphazard charity ". Every centre has its own idiosyncracies, its efficiency or otherwise depends on the man in charge at any particular time and the conduct of most of them at some times would have caused a public scandal if they had been run as public services and not as private charities. Their shortcomings have only escaped censure on the same basis as the solicitors who, having been criticized for their conduct of a Poor Person's case, received an apology the next day from the judge who explained that he had been under the impression that the solicitors were paid by the State. Some of the centres are run by political parties and are apt to flourish when elections are pending and to die away when political interest is low. At many of the well organized centres it is the practice to disclaim any liability for negligence. This is understandable from the point of view of the lawyers who are always, and especially under Poor Man's Lawyer conditions, liable to make a mistake and who would be somewhat harshly treated if they had to pay damages for a mistake in the course of work for which they were not being paid. But from the poor person's point of view he is being deprived of the normal right to be treated with reasonable professional skill and otherwise to claim damages for any loss he may suffer.

Poor Man's Lawyers have certainly made full use of the advantage enjoyed by private charitable enterprises of being free to experiment and each centre believes that its own particular system at any given moment is the best that can be devised and is jealous of any interference by, or even co-operation with, other bodies. Every possible income test, or none, is applied at some centres in England ; many of them have a rule that no letters shall be written by the advisers, or only one. Letters usually may be drafted for the applicant to copy out and sign, but even this is discouraged by the delay that will be caused and the manual labour of writing, if, as is normally the case, there is no clerk to assist with these matters. At Cambridge House at one time only barristers were allowed to advise [1]—

[1] F. C. G. Gurney Champion : op. cit.

the branch of the profession that normally has no contact with the lay client. Often if a point is difficult, the applicant, who may have waited nearly a whole week for the " P.M.L. night ", will have to wait till the following week or longer for the adviser to look the law up at his office and give him the answer. Sometimes there are too many clients to be seen and some have to be turned away. But even this is better than attempting to deal with cases at breakneck speed or advising that there is no case when really the point requires further investigation.

It is necessary to stress that this is only the debit side of the Poor Man's Lawyer Account and much of it could not be avoided in the circumstances. The men who started and persevered with these ventures have done their best, generously sacrificing their time and comfort, to give what help they could when no other help was available. Of the many thousands of cases which, collectively, they have dealt with every year, a high proportion have received all the help that was needed. It is when tested by the standards of an age which demands more than amateur first aid for the poor that they break down, and with their limited resources in men and money they could not be expected to do more than they have done.

If legal advice institutions are regarded as mere sieves, which dispose of the cases which require only a few words of explanation and pass the remainder on to another institution for litigation, the charitable systems which already exist in several large cities can be made adequate by reorganization and the expenditure of a little money. But all experience shows that more than this should be attempted. The office to which the person in legal difficulties comes for advice is the most suitable agency for carrying out negotiations and conciliations. These offices are consulted by husbands and wives half-minded to take some action of a most drastic character. It is important that their story should not be met with the attitude " Is it a divorce you want or a separation ? " Similarly there are amongst the callers people who, quite unnecessarily, wish to take action against friends and neighbours, and who require handling with tact by some local organization which they respect ; to instruct them how to apply for aid in litigation is merely to invite them to go ahead. Furthermore preventive legal advice, like preventive medicine, requires that people should be *encouraged* to seek legal advice—not merely catered for when matters have reached such a pass that they are driven to seek it. People do not realize that their problem can be solved by legal advice. Or they do realize it but do not know how they can get a lawyer's help without being treated as an object of charity. When there is no well-known, efficient and accessible centre people fall into the way of doing without lawyers and it is unnecessary to restate the undesirable consequences of this attitude. A Committee of the American Bar Association, entitled the Committee on Professional Ethics and Grievances, has ruled that publicity may be employed to tell the public why legal problems should always be taken to lawyers, that the cost of consulting a lawyer immediately the problem arises is comparatively negligible and that free and reduced-fee plans of legal aid exist. American figures show that 80 per cent. to 90 per cent. of the clients of the legal aid offices have never before consulted a lawyer.[1] It is a requirement of sound financial policy that the legal advice institution should be able to cope fully with this demand since any system of legal aid in litigation that is likely to be adopted in this country is bound to be more expensive, cumbersome, and difficult to supervise than the legal advice organization. The war, too, has shown how necessary it is that the public should be instructed in matters which vitally affect them. Consider the amount of trouble which has been spent on providing Citizens' Advice Bureaux, announcements and demonstrations by the Ministry of Food and Ministry of Health, advice on war damage and adjustment of liabilities; the same considerations of public welfare and economy make it desirable that legal advice should be provided on efficient, professional lines.

Legal advice is not, as has been suggested, the solution to the whole problem of legal aid, but it is an important part of the solution and has frequently been recognized as the basis of any satisfactory system. Moreover the foundation of some substantial institution for the purpose has frequently been advocated. In 1928 the future Lord Chancellor, then Sir Douglas Hogg, said,[2] "I should like to see the day coming when, just as medicine administers to all who need it, help for the body, so in every great centre of population we might see something akin to a legal hospital, where the poor people could rely on getting the advice and help they needed". Clearly something of this sort is required; the alternative is to give the advice at solicitors' offices

[1] Report of the American Bar Association, 1942.

[2] Quoted by P. Harrington Edwards: *The Poor and the Law in 1928*, 166 *L.T.*, 233 ff.

and no one would suggest that applicants in a well-populated area should be sent to the private offices of firms of solicitors for the sort of matters that a Poor Man's Lawyer has to deal with. More than half the enquiries can be dealt with simply at a single interview ; many of them are not strictly legal queries at all, even when they have been referred by a Citizens' Advice Bureau or social service agency ; they are matters which should be referred to the local authority or a Government Department, or for which there is no legal redress but which are worth raising with the Member of Parliament—things which a solicitor might possibly do for a private client but which the applicant can reasonably do for himself. Even in towns with a population of less than 100,000 it is doubtful whether advice at solicitors' offices will ever be a satisfactory method of dealing with these cases. The poor do not like going to a solicitor as a charity client and in some towns, where there are few solicitors compared with the density of population, if the need was really being met, clients would be trooping in every day for free advice, as can be seen from the estimate made by the American legal aid organizations that a properly run legal aid scheme should be consulted every year by one person for every hundred of the population covered.* In such towns, if the demand were not sufficient to justify a full time centre, a part-time centre could be run in conjunction with another town in the neighbourhood and for smaller towns periodical visits could be paid by the staff of the nearest advice centre, as in Sweden. This is already done by the staff of the two London Legal Advice Centres who visit outlying bureaux weekly to save the time and expense of a number of applicants who would otherwise have to travel to the centre. There is an understandable reluctance on the part of solicitors to abandon their traditional willingness to help any poor person who seeks their help, but at the same time, as the reports of Poor Persons' Committees show, they do not really like having these clients in their waiting-rooms, and complain of their manners and of the unfamiliar and distasteful nature of the work. It seems it would be better to direct the altruism of the solicitor's profession into other channels.

Clearly then legal advice centres are indicated, but there still remains the question whether advice should be given by

* Many of the legal aid offices deal with a larger proportion of the population than this ; 4·16 at Springfield is the highest ; see Smith and Bradway, op. cit., Chap. XV.

salaried advisers or by local solicitors attending in rotation with only a secretary as permanent staff. The latter is the scheme which was introduced by the Law Society for the benefit of provincial Citizens' Advice Bureaux; it was only put into operation in a few districts, and then not in its original form, but it would undoubtedly meet with greater success in peace-time. Something similar was proposed by the Haldane Society in *The Law and Reconstruction* but that proposal has been abandoned in view of the criticisms made by Dr. E. J. Cohn. It is suggested that it has nothing to recommend it except that it would be the cheapest way of doing things if, and only if, solicitors were to give their services free. The main defect of rotas is that by no means all solicitors are familiar with the branches of the law which are involved in poor persons' cases and the specialised experience of the common legal problems, of living conditions and social service agencies, which is desirable, is only slowly acquired if attendance is at infrequent intervals. Solicitors would not find it easy to attend during business hours and many matters, which in the day time could be dealt with by a telephone call to a landlord or employer or social service agency, would have to be referred to the secretary (for there would have to be a full-time secretary) or to the solicitors who undertook litigation.

That a permanent staff is an improvement on the rota system has been proved to the satisfaction of all who have taken part in the experiments at Cambridge House and the Mary Ward Settlement. To some extent the services of solicitors in private practice, who pay occasional visits to the centre, are used, but from the point of view of advising this is found to be an unsatisfactory, and sometimes dangerous, method, and one which involves so much instruction and supervision that there is very little saving of the time of the regular staff.

There are people who for many years have devoted their energies to Poor Man's Lawyer, or similar, work and who resent the introduction of professionalism into what has become for them a hobby and a source of understandable pride. They maintain that everything is done for the poor that is necessary, or, if it is not, only a little reorganization is needed without disturbing the philanthropic basis of the work. For them the lines of Tennyson might have been written:

> The old order changeth, yielding place to new
> And God fulfils himself in many ways,
> Lest one good custom should corrupt the world.

There is a great difference between work done as a favour by an unpaid volunteer and work done by a professional man employed for those duties. The old system might conceivably be made adequate for the giving of advice pure and simple ; it can never be satisfactory if the larger purposes of legal aid centres are to be achieved.

CHAPTER XII

FURTHER ASSISTANCE

As has been pointed out, a considerable number of applicants require not only legal advice, but assistance in negotiation or conciliation, while a few cases require court proceedings. There is also a small, legitimate demand for non-contentious work, such as wills in respect of small estates, administrations, leases and mortgages. How is this assistance to be rendered?

It would undoubtedly be simplest for the centres, or a department of which they were a branch, both to give advice and conduct any necessary business including legal proceedings. Whether or not you approve of such a solution depends in the last resort on whether you approve of "bureaucracy" in general and "bureaucracy" in legal matters in particular. An overwhelming majority of the legal profession is wholeheartedly opposed to anything to which the word "officialism" might be applied, and it has sufficient sympathizers to be bound to succeed in its opposition, if such a solution can possibly be avoided. Quite apart from the lack of enterprise and efficiency which is associated with a public office there is the strong argument that if the idea of a legal aid department caught hold it might challenge the independence of the legal profession which constitutes such an important factor in the fight for the rights of the individual against the encroachments of the State.

It should be pointed out that the Advice Centres which we have just discussed are not necessarily public offices in the sense that they are under the control of the Government or even of local authorities. In the U.S.A. in 1933 there were eighty-four or more legal aid organizations,[1] employing an aggregate full-time staff of at least eighty-one lawyers, seventy clerks and twenty-five investigators, but there were only ten municipal or State legal aid bureaux.[2] The question of whether the Government or some other body should control the bureaux and the legal aid scheme in general is dealt with in Chapter XIV. At the moment we are only concerned with the question of whether poor persons' cases should be conducted by private firms of solicitors or not, but the

[1] R. Heber Smith and Bradway: *The Growth of Legal Aid Work in the U.S.*, Chap. XIV. In 1941 there were 143 organizations.
[2] Ibid., Chap. XVI.

issue has become confused because it has been represented that the only alternative would be a Government department.

It is important that our consideration of the problem should not be affected by irrelevant motives and arguments. The story of legal aid reform makes disturbing reading from this point of view. Some of the lapses of the first Lawrence Committee have already been mentioned but they are surpassed by the arguments used against the proposal to establish an office for the conduct of poor persons' matrimonial cases: "As regards matrimonial cases, the official would in most cases have to undertake the impossible task of acting on both sides. Two officials would have to be constituted, one for Petitioners and the other for Respondents." [1] This impossible task has been quietly and efficiently accomplished during the war in this country, as it was in Sweden and parts of the U.S.A. many years ago. The argument continues:

> If an official or officials were established, there would be no efficient check on the question of means and the result might be that many small cases would be conducted at the expense of the country where the litigants were able to pay the ordinary costs. Moreover, if a Government Department for this purpose were once established, it would be an easy matter for the Government of the day to increase the limit as to means and thus undertake cases which solicitors and barristers would ordinarily undertake at a reasonable profit.
>
> In our opinion it would be far better (so long at all events as there is no public fund out of which to defray the costs of Poor Persons' litigation) to allow the work to be done by private practitioners, who would have the greatest interest in seeing that the privileges granted to Poor Persons were not abused.

It is hard to see why an official should not be competent and conscientious enough to check the means of applicants but it is almost incredible that a committee appointed by the Lord Chancellor should argue that legal aid should be left to private solicitors in order that they should be able to prevent a Government from injuring the interests of the profession by deciding that legal aid was needed in more cases.

These absurdities are not quoted in order to poke fun at the Committee. Times have changed greatly, and it is no longer necessary to demonstrate the inadequacies of the Report. But the legal profession has a long memory and arguments which have once been put forward in an authoritative form are apt to stick. There are strong arguments against a Government department

[1] Cmd. 430.

but these are not the ones. The 1925 Report [1] laid its finger on the spot when it pointed out that it would be difficult for the valuable relationship between solicitor and client to survive if there were a Government office. It is hard to say just what constitutes this relationship : it is certainly not, as the Report suggests, that the client would have more confidence in the skill and honesty of a private solicitor. Perhaps the most one can say is that it is a personal relationship, as opposed to an official relationship. It is very doubtful how far this ideal is attained by the present Poor Persons' Procedure or by Poor Man's Lawyer Centres, or whether any adequate service can be organized sufficiently cheaply without injuring the relationship.

According to the 1925 Report : "If the scheme proposed in this Report should fail to prove effective it is difficult to see what alternative would then be available except the institution of a State Department, however objectionable on other grounds such a measure may be, and in that event the question of the institution of a State system will require further consideration."

The scheme has, under the stress of new conditions and conceptions, proved inadequate even in the limited field which it covered and extension to other matters and to more people is necessary. Nevertheless it may still not be inevitable that all legal aid work should be undertaken by a department, much less a State department : there is still the possibility of better co-operation between the State and the profession. Let us ascertain what are the difficulties of organization with regard to the reforms which have been indicated as being necessary and, bearing in mind general principles as well as immediate expediency, endeavour to arrive at a solution.

The alternative to the Advice Centres providing assistance beyond advice is that the cases should be referred to private firms of solicitors. We have already said that solicitors cannot and should not take up these cases gratuitously—it is inevitable that they would be neglected. If on the other hand, reasonable payment was made to the solicitors the cases would on the whole be dealt with as well as at a centre although the staff of the centre would naturally gain a very thorough experience of certain types of cases. But the system raises a difficulty. If the solicitor is to be paid according to the amount of work he does on a case, which is the accepted method of payment, he will be tempted to conduct the case in a lavish manner, knowing that his fees will

[1] Cmd. 2358.

be paid from public funds. This is to some extent the risk in a private case but where fees are being paid by the client his consideration for his own pocket does act as a check on unnecessary expenditure ; the assisted client, however, will naturally be only too anxious to have his case dealt with in the greatest possible detail and for some outside body to scrutinize a solicitor's bill to see whether any unnecessary work has been done would be difficult and distasteful.

One solution which has been suggested is that a fixed sum should be paid to a solicitor for each case that he undertakes, so much for an undefended divorce, so much for an accident case. This is what is done under the present system of legal aid in criminal cases and, although it would be much more complicated in civil cases having regard to the greater variety and the possibility of settlement at different stages of the proceedings, it would be possible to work out a scale of some kind, but it would work in a very rough and ready fashion and it would give the solicitor no incentive to do his work thoroughly.

On the other hand there is a great deal to be said for the centre conducting negotiations and proceedings. In the first place if the centre staff were to do nothing but give one interview to each applicant, advise him, and, if more was needed, refer him to a solicitor, it would be a very uninteresting job for a qualified professional man and the work would suffer. Then a certain amount of investigation is necessary to decide whether the applicant has any need of a solicitor's services. The writing of a single letter may elicit the fact that the applicant is mistaken as to the facts of the matter and has no case whatever. Also the bureau would undoubtedly be able to do the work of negotiation for less than a private solicitor could economically charge. Above all the Centre would be more interested in getting the matter settled without court proceedings and would probably, by gaining a reputation for impartiality and helpfulness to all parties, be in a better position to do so than a private solicitor who is inevitably partisan. The New York and other American Legal Aid Societies write to the opposing parties, interview both parties and in many cases send out investigators to interview the witnesses and obtain evidence as to facts and character. Mr. R. H. Smith wrote : " The Legal Aid Societies whose offices in America are just like any ordinary private law office have earned such a reputation for fair dealing that the opposing party is often willing to come and relate his story. The legal aid lawyer changes his attitude from that of advocate to that of arbitrator." It is only through this same confidence in his fairness that the English Poor Man's Lawyer has been able to deal with many of the cases on which he has been consulted and when he has failed it has usually been due to lack of time and facilities to conduct the investigations and negotiations thoroughly.

There are overwhelming considerations in favour of the centres being equipped to conduct negotiations ; it is not essential that they should actually act in the place of solicitors in court proceedings. It would, however, be perfectly possible for them to do so, just as the Services Divorce Department conducts divorce cases, and it is questionable whether the Government would agree to pay private firms of solicitors reasonable remuneration for conducting litigation when the work could be done more cheaply by the centres. The Services Divorce Department is able to carry divorce cases through for a little over 3 guineas a time (excluding court fees and disbursements), as compared with £60 or £70 for the simplest case privately conducted. Probably the most convenient arrangement in practice would be for this Department to be extended so that it could deal with all High Court matters, while the centres conducted litigation in the inferior courts.

At the same time consideration must be given to the effect on the relationship between solicitor and client of allowing cases to be conducted in this way and in any event an applicant should be entitled to insist on his case being conducted by a private solicitor if he prefers it. As Dr. Cohn says, there should be no monopoly of legal aid.[1] There are also the considerations that the applicant may have had his own solicitor before his poverty became acute, or he may have a low opinion of the centre, or it may be acting for another interested party. In every law suit there is usually at least one disgruntled party ; it is very important that he should not be able to blame the system for having forced on him a representative he did not want. Dr. Cohn points out that this choice exists in Sweden and has been found to " stimulate a competition of helpfulness " between the bureaux and the private firms. It will involve more expense if the private firm is to receive reasonable fees and there is the difficulty of supervising the solicitor's bills. It has, however, been said that in Sweden 90 per cent. of applicants prefer to be represented by the bureaux.[2]

[1] 59 *L.Q.R.*, 267.
[2] F. C. G. Gurney Champion, *Justice and the Poor in England.*

It is thought that with this safeguard the Legal Advice Centres or, as they would more appropriately be called, Legal Aid Centres, would relieve solicitors of a burden rather than rob them of a privilege. They might then incidentally provide a solution for the problem which is constantly causing difficulty in the legal profession, that of education. The Poor Persons' Procedure has sometimes been described as helping in the education of young barristers and that is, in fact, the main reason why, so far as counsel are concerned, there has been no difficulty in getting volunteers. The practice in this respect cannot be other than condemned. For an untried barrister to be entrusted with a case which is dependent on skilful presentation, merely because he has volunteered and is next on the list, is a striking instance of the treatment of poor litigants. But barristers and solicitors, like doctors, must acquire experience ; the obvious course is that they should acquire it by working under supervision and the Legal Aid Centre would be an alternative or supplementary training for those who do not prefer, or who are unable to afford, to be articled to a solicitor or to work in a barrister's chambers.* The practice has been developed in many countries and particularly in America where it forms part of the curriculum at some Law Schools.[1] It is pointed out that it not only provides a supply of trained legal aid workers but gives many members of the legal profession the perspective and " ethical idealism "[2] which comes from practical experience of work of this kind.

A network of Legal Aid Centres is, then, the basic structure of the proposed scheme for legal aid. They would be run much on the lines of an ordinary office with a sufficient qualified staff of solicitors, managing clerks and clerical workers. Having regard to the division of the legal profession it would probably be considered more suitable to instruct outside barristers in the ordinary way, but there would be either on the staff, or closely co-operating with the centre, trained social workers. In this way not only would competent advice be made available but thorough negotiation and conciliation would be carried out to the benefit of society in general and the amount of litigation would be kept down to a minimum while no one need be deprived in the last resort of the amenities provided by the courts.

* In the case of the Bar, training at a Centre would not, of course, take the place of experience in a barrister's chambers but would be supplementary to it.

[1] These institutions were favourably mentioned in the Report of the Special Committee of the American Bar Association on Low Cost Legal Service Bureaux, 1942.

[2] R. Heber Smith and Bradway, op. cit., Chap. XVIII.

So far in this chapter we have been concerned with the position of applicants who could afford to pay only a nominal fee, or none at all, but there would still be the clients whose means bring them just above this level and who require partial assistance as much as the lowest group requires full assistance. In several countries the free legal aid system covers such people with the simple difference that they pay a proportion of the usual legal charges. In the U.S.A. a special committee on " Low Cost Legal Service Bureaux " appointed by the American Bar Association, which reported in 1942, was not in favour of this service being combined with that of Legal Aid Bureaux acting for no charge whatever. The reason given, that it would lead to confusion between the two services, one based on charity and the other on limited compensation, is somewhat vague, but there is a good practical reason for a different system in that it is desirable to disturb the solicitor and client relationship as little as possible and the dangers of subsidizing solicitors to take assisted cases do not apply when the client is himself paying part of the fees.

Three of the methods of dealing with these cases which are in use in America were recommended by the Bar Association's Committee. One of these referred to bureaux run in conjunction with Law Schools and need not concern us here. The other two were as follows :

1. " The neighbourhood law office plan." This plan appears to be nothing more than a suggestion that firms should run branch offices in outlying districts at which moderate fees, fixed and payable in advance, would enable the solicitor to make some profit, while encouraging people of small means to overcome their fear of high legal charges. The Committee itself said : " We would hesitate to recommend it standing alone."

2. " The Lawyers' Reference Plan." The idea here is a central office which would be publicized. The office would have a list of lawyers who had volunteered to act, on demand, at fixed modest fees and who had accepted the conditions that they would report to the central office the result of cases and the amount of fees collected and would submit any disputes with their referred clients to some agency selected by the central office.

The Central Office would be suitably situated at the offices of the Bar Association, at the municipal courts, or elsewhere. The fees, according to the Committee's recommendation, should be just enough to defray the actual expense of conducting the plan and the profit motive should be eliminated. Fees should be standardized and for advice might be based on the time consumed. Under the plan operating in Chicago the charges are $3.00 for a first consultation up to half an hour, $5.00 for an hour ; for court work a maximum of $5.00 per day or appearance.

The Committee stressed that " the plan proposed would make no inroads on the present income of practising attorneys. Even if that were not so we would still urge action . . . in the belief that it would be an outstanding contribution to the public welfare " and again " The resulting good will toward the bar will be almost inestimable ".

There is no question about the goodwill nor about the finding of the Committee that 80 per cent. to 90 per cent. of the clients using the reference plan had never before consulted a lawyer but it is doubtful whether the legal profession in this country would agree to eliminate the profit motive in this class of case or whether they should be asked to do so. At the same time it is not to be expected that full professional fees would be paid and the fear is sometimes expressed that the acceptance of reduced fees would lead to the idea that scale fees are too high and that solicitors can afford to work for less. This is quite a separate question. The average income of solicitors is said to be very moderate ; their fees are regulated by a statutory committee and this should be an adequate safeguard. The fact that a slight increase of fees was granted in 1943 points to the fact that their fees are not too high. In 1930 the report of a committee of the Chamber of Commerce into the cost of legal proceedings was that " the net income of the average legal practitioners, in the interests of the public, should not be reduced, having regard to the high standard of education and probity required in the legal profession, the long period of waiting before earning a living wage and the strict supervision exercised over the barristers and solicitors, especially the latter ".[1]

There is really no reason why lawyers should not receive a fair profit from any work which they undertake. If, owing to the number or simplicity of the cases, they can afford to deal with poor persons' cases at a lower rate, so much the better ; they will in any event be expected to do so, and for many reasons it will probably pay them in the long run. In the first place it will help to stop the rot that has set in—the constant loss of legal business to banks, accountants and other specialists and the cutting out of lawyers by personal application departments, administra-

[1] Quoted by Mr. Mullins : *In Quest of Justice.*

tive tribunals and arbitration proceedings. Some of these tendencies may be inevitable and right but it cannot be denied that the legal profession will be benefitting itself by providing a reasonable alternative, and may be helping to solve the unemployment problem which afflicts it in peace time. The new business would provide some profit even when reduced fees were being charged ; the public would learn to rely on lawyers instead of fighting shy of them, and assisted persons who later became more wealthy would continue to employ those whom they had learnt to value in their early days.

There is, then, no objection to less than the usual remuneration being paid provided that the fees are sufficient to ensure an adequate supply of willing solicitors and barristers, and the legal aid centre need not deal with these reduced fee cases at all, except, possibly, such of them as require only advice or information and can be disposed of at a single interview.

The most rational method of paying for cases which are being assisted either in whole or in part would be to decide what proportion of scale fees solicitors ought to receive. Let us say two-thirds is the proportion decided upon. First of all the amount which the assisted person could himself afford to contribute would be assessed from his declaration or from the certificate supplied by the Inspector of Taxes or Social Welfare Officer. It is desirable that the applicant should know his exact liability and should be asked to find a fixed sum if possible, on the other hand there are some cases in which it is equally desirable that he should be in the same position as any other client and should have to pay proportionately for extra thoroughness or difficulty. If costs were not recovered from the opposing party the solicitor would receive the contribution, if any, due from his client, and the balance would be paid out of the funds of the legal aid organization to make the remuneration up to two-thirds of scale fees. Barristers' fees would be fixed by arrangement with the Bar Council.

As has been said this would be the most rational method of payment. Solicitors' fees are fixed by a statutory body so that it is already decided what charges are reasonable for ordinary work ; it is thus easy to say that a certain reduction must be made for public work and to fix the proportion of scale fees at an appropriate level. Two-thirds might be considered too high from the point of view of the expense involved, in which case it would be reduced, but the method suggested would have the great advantage of keeping the same principle of payment for work done as in ordinary cases. The solicitors' method of charging has been much criticized and is due to come up for review after the war; it may be that a better system will then be adopted but it is doubtful whether in the meantime there is any advantage in departing from it in respect of assisted cases.

If, however, the legal aid organization's finances did not justify the acceptance of this unknown liability another solution would have to be adopted. It is not sufficient to allow the solicitor only such costs as he can succeed in recovering from the opposing party because he would then be reluctant to undertake cases which did not promise a good chance of success and he would be over anxious to get cases settled for fear they should be lost if fought to a finish and no costs recovered, apart from the amount, if any, which his own client could contribute. He should at least be guaranteed a fixed sum for each case even if it is unsuccessful and whether his client is being wholly or partially assisted. Of course if the sum were less than the party and party costs would come to, there would still be the temptation to settle too easily and, in any event, the less work that had to be done the better for the solicitor, so that the less promising and more troublesome cases would not be welcomed. The only way to deal with this would be to provide some extra reward for extra trouble, which is, in effect, what the present system of solicitors' remuneration does.

CHAPTER XIII

FINANCE

Having gone thus far it may be useful to review the principles and conclusions which have emerged from the preceding chapters. For a statement of general principles it is difficult to improve on the three main points laid down in a paper [1] read to the International Law Association in 1901, and subsequently endorsed by that Association :

1. All courts of every country should be open to all persons notwithstanding their poverty or nationality.
2. Where lack of means prevents litigation on the usual conditions these should be relaxed and the way provided whereby a poor person can prosecute or defend a claim and obtain justice.
3. In every populous place or seat of a court of justice free legal advice from properly qualified lawyers should be obtainable by persons unable to pay for it.

How far are these principles observed in this country?

We have seen that in England after a chequered history a system of legal aid has been arrived at which is administered by the solicitors' profession and which depends upon the voluntary and gratuitous services of that profession and of the Bar. The Poor Persons' Procedure referred to applies only to the High Court and the Court of Appeal. In view of the fact that a Poor Person may have to find a deposit of £5 or £20, or, in exceptional cases, even more, it is clear that any destitute person is excluded from the scheme, and in view of the fact that a person with over £4 a week, or over £100 worth of capital assets of all kinds, cannot in any circumstances take advantage of the procedure, but must pay the ordinary fees of the court and of solicitors and barristers, it is equally clear that there are many people who need some degree of legal aid who are not yet provided for.

As regards the County Court and civil cases in the Police Court no official legal aid is provided apart from remission of court fees in the Police Court, but a number of organizations, charitable or otherwise, attempt to tackle the problem so far as representation and the provision of disbursements are concerned. Representation is provided by an entirely different, and paid, system in criminal cases, and strong criticism has been directed

[1] By J. P. Coldstream, W.S.

against the operation of this system in the magistrates' courts. No representation or assistance with expenses is provided in the House of Lords.

Legal advice is provided by a large number of separate organizations on a charitable basis. Advice centres vary widely in every respect and could undoubtedly be improved both in methods and organization. In a large proportion of cases advice is being given by unqualified persons and, not only in rural areas but also in large cities, the schemes which exist are quite inadequate to do all the work necessary in this direction.

In short the fundamental requirements for justice as understood in a democracy are not being observed and it is suggested that the following reforms are necessary:

1. Power to remit court fees in the County Court and to provide representation by a solicitor, and sometimes counsel, in the County Court and Police Court.
2. In all courts a more generous and more pliable test of means and provisions for partial legal aid.
3. In all courts power to provide assistance with disbursements and expert evidence, including the preparation of cases.
4. Authority to decide applications for legal aid should be derived from the court and be subject to its control.
5. The liability for costs in assisted cases should be substantially the same as in ordinary cases.
6. Efficient and thorough legal advice should be available throughout the country and this involves the setting up of legal advice centres in large towns at least.
7. The question should be considered of including criminal proceedings, House of Lords and Privy Council appeals, and bankruptcy within the same scheme. In any event some method of ensuring that legal aid certificates are more frequently granted in Police Court trials is required.

A considerable amount of agreement is found among Poor Man's Lawyers on the points summarized above but, while it is easy for those who have had first-hand experience to see what needs to be done, there is a considerable variety of suggestions as to how it should be done. Fundamentally the differences of opinion arise from the question whether lawyers should give their services free or not. It is obvious that if payment were forthcoming for the services which are required there would be no great difficulty in organizing a scheme to provide for all points but, in legal circles particularly, the idea is dying hard that legal aid should be dependent on the charity of the legal profession.

This argument is frequently supported by a comparison with the services given by doctors to the hospitals and a scheme—quite a far-reaching scheme—for " Law Hospitals " was outlined in a paper [1] read at the 11th annual meeting of the Law Society in 1884. Even then it was not suggested that all the work would be done free, but in any event the anology between the medical and solicitor's professions is unsound. The doctor who gives his services to a hospital is enabled to do so because he is entitled to charge his private patients large and uncontrolled fees, whereas the solicitors' fees are restricted ; it can even be said that a doctor is able to obtain such large fees because of the standing which he gains from being attached to a hospital. He also gains experience in the hospital which is valuable to him in his private practice and—a minor point—he owes his early training to experience gained in this public institution and might therefore, be said to have a duty to repay the benefits received. Moreover, it is not the rank and file of the medical profession who are expected to give their services ; the consultants are eminent and established men while the general practitioner is not expected to do more than accept panel cases or waive his charges in individual cases, if he feels so inclined. Conditions are utterly different so far as the solicitor is concerned and indeed there is no other profession which provides organized charity on a large scale.

There need be no competition in philanthropy between the medical and legal professions ; the fact is clear, and there are good reasons for it, that the system of Hospital consultants works, while any scheme which depends upon the unpaid services of solicitors does not. In spite of repeated efforts by the Law Societies and considerable altruism on the part of some solicitors it has not been possible to implement fully even the existing Poor Persons' Rules, which cover only a small percentage of the needs of the poor—2¼ per cent. according to Mr. Harrington Edwards's estimate [2]—of which the great majority are undefended divorces. Professor Keeton suggests [3] that probably for each case brought there is at least one other which had a reasonable chance of success, and which was brought to the notice of local committees, and many times that number not brought to the attention of committees at all. This comment, which is based largely on the fact that

[1] By F. W. Blunt. [2] *The Poor and the Law in 1928*, 166 *L.T.*, 233.
[3] G. W. Keeton : *Law Reform after the War*, 58 *L.Q.R.*, 254 (1942).

97 per cent. of poor persons' cases are successful, possibly does not take account of the fact that a large number of the cases are undefended divorce suits, but the general conclusion is perfectly true that, in spite of increased activity, the work discharged, compared with the work that ought to be done, is still very small.

It is frequently stated that the assistance given in poor persons' cases is as good as work done for paying clients. If this were so the legal profession would be immune from the frailities of human nature which afflict the rest of mankind. Solicitors have fairly heavy office expenses which have to be met just the same while poor persons' cases are being conducted and these are in many offices handed over to articled or junior clerks working without adequate supervision and are put on one side when there is pressure of business. Young and briefless barristers are only too willing to conduct cases for nothing, but when they are beginning to make careers for themselves, their clerks are not so anxious for them to accept this work. It must be remembered that there is no selection of suitable barristers or solicitors. Any offers are gladly accepted and, while there are many men and women in both branches of the profession who give of their very best, there are also volunteers who have only been induced by the constant pressure of their law society and considerations of prestige to put their names on the rota, as well as some who are just bad lawyers. One is reminded of the story of the young counsel who, having thoroughly mishandled his case, could get no further in his closing speech than "My Lord, my poor client . . . my poor client . . ." "Pray continue, Mr. ——," said the judge, "so far, the court is entirely with you."

Dependence on the charity of the profession inevitably involves excessive regard for the interests of the profession. As Gurney Champion wrote:

> Every precaution seems to have been taken to prevent any abuses by the profession, to preserve their privileges except as to any right to remuneration, and to restrict as much as possible the legal aid given, both as to its character and as to the classes of persons who were to receive it. In no sense do these rules give anything else to the poor than legal charity, restricted and hedged round by rules which do not apply to ordinary litigants. Any legal aid given is merely a matter of discretion.

Yet, as Professor Keeton says,[1] "It may be questioned if, in the strenuous world into which we are passing, even the present

[1] 58 *L.Q.R.*, 254.

modest scheme of aid can be maintained indefinitely on the present basis." Even before the present war it had broken down again in Wales and it had broken down in other parts of the country in so far as the committees regulated the number of certificates granted by the number of conducting solicitors available and excluded applicants on the grounds of merit and the means of their relatives.

If the profession could not cope with the obligations they had accepted they obviously could not contemplate any extension of those obligations by allowing the Poor Persons' Rules to be extended and, in particular, the financial limits raised as the value of money declined. Even in a long and enlightened article in the *Law Journal* in 1925,[1] after saying that the financial limits (still in force twenty years later) were no longer adequate, the writer continues, "At the same time it is very necessary that the limit of means should not be fixed too high if the services of the profession are to be given gratuitously," and some years later the Law Society gave evidence before the Finlay Committee that there was no need for legal aid in the County and Police Courts.[2] Legal advice, too, while recognized as highly important, received no official support apart from verbal encouragement.

The crux of the matter is this : it is not a question of keeping going the present limited scheme of aid in the High Court, it is a question of vastly extending the scope of those provisions ; the need for this cannot be ignored and it is absolutely clear that it cannot be done by the gratuitous services of the legal profession.

Solicitors and barristers have themselves been firm upholders of the principle that there should be no payment for work done for poor persons. They have willingly accepted pronouncements from committees and other bodies that it is their duty to render honorary services to the poor. These invocations are usually made on the basis that the legal profession has a monopoly of the practice of the law but that is simply to say that, for the benefit of the public, only people who are properly trained are to be allowed to conduct certain kinds of business. That does not constitute a privilege in return for which certain free services must be rendered. What it does mean is that lawyers, who alone can appreciate fully the need for their services, must see that their services are made available to all ; but because the law costs more than many people can afford to pay, lawyers should not have to bear the whole burden of remedying that particular result of

[1] 60 *L.J.*, 213, 237, 261

[2] Annual Report, 1927.

poverty, any more than milk retailers must provide free milk to children because children need milk and cannot afford it. Clearly the responsibility rests upon the State, as representative of the whole community. The *Law Journal* in 1914 said of the new system which had just been introduced,[1] "It is primarily a recognition by the State of its obligations to persons who are too poor to assert or defend their rights in the courts in the ordinary way," and looked forward to further developments. In 1924 we find in the same journal [2]: "The English system is largely unsatisfactory because it imposes upon solicitors, however keen their sense of civic duty may be, a burden which they cannot reasonably be expected to bear," and "In England, as in Scotland, no system of legal assistance is at all likely to be successful until the State does recognize its responsibility in the matter." From the time when the Law Society took control, however, there is a noticeable reluctance to admit that the system is not all that it might be or that there is any need for its extension to other courts and to legal advice.

In the past when the problem was very much smaller and there was a reasonable prospect of coping with it by charity it was commendable on the part of the legal profession that they felt that the social responsibilities of a profession demanded free service to the poor, but when voluntary services have been proved to be inadequate a different method of working has to be adopted.

As was said in a paper read at the International Conference on Legal Aid Work held at Geneva in 1924 [3]:

> However high the bar's standard may be—and it is very high—it has not moral strength to struggle for any length of time against the law of recompense for human activity; and if, taken all together, the system of free help does not measure up to those social exigencies to which one would wish to apply it, this is not to be laid to the attorneys, but exclusively to the illusion of the legislator who believes he can solve a serious problem with fine words: as by announcing that this free help is an "honourable activity" of the legal profession.

There is no need for lawyers to feel that they will be accused of looking for more business if they stress the necessity of some payment for these cases—they have stood out against this innovation for too long for that—nor need they feel that payment on less than the usual scale will lower the standing of the profession.

[1] 49 *L.J.*, 362. [2] 59 *L.J.*, 415.

[3] By Silvio Longhi, first President of the Court of Appeal. Quoted in *Growth of Legal Aid Work in the United States.*

Collectively the legal profession cannot be said to stand as high in the eyes of the public as it should. That is no doubt partly because lawyers are unfairly blamed for the law being what it is but they would be very much more respected * if they provided, for reasonable remuneration, a service to everybody who needed it rather than attempted to provide inadequate services at their own cost.

If it is accepted that far-reaching reforms are necessary and that these can only be carried out by providing reasonable remuneration for services, we still have to consider how the money is to be found.

The scheme should, of course, be made self-supporting as far as possible, by charging fees for advice and services when the applicants can afford to pay anything at all and by appropriating costs recovered from opposing parties. The controversy which took place among the American organizations as to whether charges should be made reveals that the arguments against this course are either excessively forward-looking, namely that justice should be entirely free, or appropriate only to an era that has passed, namely that it is more dignified and more appreciated if no charge is made. On the other side it is pointed out that the requirement of a small application fee eliminates fictitious and groundless complaints, proves that the client is in earnest, enables him to feel that he is not asking for charity, and helps the funds. In 1936 fifteen of the American organizations charged an application fee, while thirty-six did not.[1] Needless to say there must be power to remit any charges which may be fixed, so as not to exclude completely destitute applicants.

In so far as the scheme is not self-supporting there are a number of alternative methods one or more of which might be employed to raise the money. The first source to which the Government would naturally look is charitable subscribers, but unfortunately legal aid work does not appeal sufficiently to the general public. It is difficult to explain the value of the work to someone who has little knowledge of law and legal procedure and even in America, where private legal aid organizations have been

* The prestige accruing from the legal aid service has been recognized by many of the United States Bar Association. John S. Bradway, Director of the Legal Aid Clinic, Duke University, writes: "The Legal Aid organization is generally recognized as a humanitarian plank in the public relations programme of the organized bar. For the community it is an agency which relates the functions of the lawyer to those of the social worker and the representatives of other professional groups." 24 *Jo. of Comparative Legislation*, 1942, pp. 49 ff.

[1] R. Heber Smith and Bradway: *Growth of Legal Aid Work in the United States.*

much more successful than in this country, it has been found that the work does not receive the support of large charitable subscribers and it is always hampered by lack of funds.[1] In this country Poor Man's Lawyers have seldom succeeded in maintaining an independent existence for long and continuity has only been maintained when this important work was sheltered under the wing of a Law Society or social service organization. As a small part of a larger charitable organization it does not receive the attention which it requires, while lawyers have their own reasons for restricting any developments of legal aid schemes. Dependence on charitable subscriptions would, as in the past, mean shortage of funds.

One of the possible methods of raising funds which deserves most careful consideration is insurance. Sir William Beveridge says in his report on Social Security [2]: "The first view is that benefit in return for contributions, rather than free allowances from the State, is what the people of Britain desire. This desire is shown both by the established popularity of compulsory insurance and the phenomenal growth of voluntary insurance against sickness, against death, and for endowment, and most recently for hospital treatment." So far as legal aid is concerned the idea of insurance has had few supporters. Voluntary insurance is clearly not feasible and no genuine scheme has ever been attempted although sometimes the fiction of membership subscriptions has been employed by legal aid societies with commercial objects. The fact is that one just does not budget for legal expenses ; the risk is not sufficiently high to justify voluntary insurance and any attempt to pay for legal aid by contributions in advance would have to be compulsory.

The proposal was made to the Finlay Committee that the National Health Insurance Acts should be extended to provide legal aid. It is doubtful whether at the present date the principle of the panel system would have many advocates. Complaints are made against it, so far as it concerns doctors, that it encourages a doctor to get the maximum number of patients on his panel, so that he may receive the capitation fees, while providing him with no incentive to give his best attention to patients when they are ill. It is thought by lawyers to be a certain way of lowering the standards of the profession and it seems particularly unsuited to the law, the whole machinery of which is based upon the desirability of preventing unnecessary litigation.

[1] R. H. Smith : *Justice and the Poor.*

[2] Cmd. 6404, para. 21.

But a compulsory insurance scheme does not necessarily mean that the capitation fee and panel system must be adopted ; it is possible to decide on the best form of organization of legal advice and assistance and merely to use the insurance principle as a method of providing the funds for maintaining the organization. Thus by the payment of a barely noticeable addition to the contributions proposed in the Beveridge Scheme a thorough going legal aid scheme could be financed. The question is whether legal aid is the type of need for which the potential beneficiaries should pay in advance or not.* It would mean that a large number of people would pay contributions without ever receiving the benefit. This again would mean that people, conscious of having paid their contributions, would feel justified in making use of the facilities on trivial matters. The poorest people would not be able to pay contributions at all and it would seem more in line with the general practice if those who could afford to pay something should pay when they receive the benefits and thus be subject to the same deterrent as the ordinary client.

We thus come to what seems to most people to be the obvious and right method of financing legal aid, that is, that the State should make itself responsible for providing the necessary funds, in so far as the scheme is not made self-supporting by the contributions of the assisted persons and their opponents.

The extent to which the State makes itself responsible for the cost of the judicial system as a whole is a matter of policy. In this country, court fees in the Supreme Court are paid on the basis that the judges' salaries and pensions should be paid out of public funds and that all other expenses of the court should be paid by suitors.† So far as the County Courts are concerned the Treasury accepts responsibility for the salaries, pensions and travelling expenses of the judges and also for the cost of court buildings. There is nothing sacred in this division of the financial burden and if it is found that new additions to the judicial machinery are necessary, and there is no other reasonable way of providing them, the cost must fall upon the Treasury. The cost of the administrative machinery of the Poor Persons' Procedure has already been accepted and it is now a question of extending the services which are no longer adequate.

The fear that the provision of funds by the Treasury would

* Under the Beveridge Scheme, of course, very substantial contributions are also made by employers and the State, but this does not affect the point I am discussing here.

† See R. M. Jackson : *The Machinery of Justice in England*, pp. 239–41. On this basis there was a "profit" in 1937 and this was still the case in 1941–2.

mean control of the legal profession by the Government is unreasonable. Many public services are dependant on Government grants but are free from interference within the proper sphere of their activity. Examples in the realm of social service are Citizens' Advice Bureaux and Youth Clubs. The Government has for the last three years contributed £25,000 a year for Citizens' Advice Bureaux. The Central Citizens' Advice Bureaux Committee has a Grants Committee on which the Ministry of Health is represented and the Ministry makes certain conditions under which the grant has to be administered. Apart from that there is no control over the work of the Bureaux. Similarly many Youth Clubs run by settlements or other voluntary social service bodies receive substantial grants from the Board of Education towards salaries, equipment and other expenses without any interference with the management of the clubs. The integrity of the organizations and a right of inspection are the sole guarantees that the money will be properly applied. Another example is provided by the Friends' Committee for Refugees and Aliens. Here the Government makes a grant to cover 100 per cent. of the cost of maintenance of refugees where the payments do not exceed individual assessments made by the Assistance Board, and of 75 per cent. of other expenses such as administrative, medical and communal welfare expenses. The grant is administered by a Central Committee on which there is no Government representation. If the Government is prepared to leave the administration of its grants to voluntary social service agencies in these matters there is no reason to believe that it would attempt to interfere in legal matters. The question of control is, however, dealt with in the next chapter. For the time being the material point is that funds could be provided by the Government without affecting the independence of the legal profession.

There is no reason to think that the amount of the grant which would be required would alarm a Treasury accustomed to the expenditure of the last few years and committed to a large expenditure on social services in the future.* Citizens' Advice Bureaux do already receive substantial grants from the Government and legal aid, a vital part of the machinery of justice, has more than an equal claim. There are other conceivable sources of contribution which we have not yet explored because they are

* As a rough indication of the relative cost of legal aid see Chap. VI, p. 46, where it is shown that in Sweden the cost to the State of the legal aid scheme was $\frac{1}{360}$th of the total State expenditure for social purposes.

not considered of major importance. For the sake of completemess, however, they may be included.

One is the possibility that the opponent of an assisted person, if unsuccessful, should make an extra payment to the funds of the legal aid organization over and above the costs for which he is made liable. This could not possibly be required unless the organization guaranteed the payment of the opponent's costs if he was successful. It might then be argued that since he had a better chance of recovering his costs than in an ordinary case if he was successful, he should be subject to a higher expense if he was unsuccessful. Another minor source would be a tax on any sums recovered in the proceedings by assisted persons. It is already the case that assisted persons may be ordered to pay costs out of sums recovered but the present suggestion is that a further sum should be paid where circumstances justified it, to the funds of the organization which assisted the recovery. This, however, would be a very rough and ready rule since most of the benefits provided by the scheme would be divorces and the recovery of personal property or small sums which would not justify any contribution being levied, and there would be very few beneficiaries who could be called upon to contribute. The final possible source of finance, namely the local authorities, is only suggested by the fact that the ratepayers bear the cost of the defence of poor prisoners in this country. A similar proposal was considered by the Scottish Committee and the conclusion was reached,[1] on the authority of the statement that "Scots Law regarded the protection of individuals from injury as one of the main objects of Civil Government", that any expense in criminal cases should form a charge upon the Treasury. It is difficult to see any reason other than financial expediency for calling upon local funds for legal aid in criminal or civil cases.

The old idea of individual charity is fast being superceded by the more modern, yet no less ethical, conception of the responsibility of the community for all its members. Necessary social services are no longer the exclusive preserve of philanthropic institutions ; they are becoming part of the fabric of the State itself and their provision is regarded as a duty of the community as a whole. Thus, in the sphere of legal aid it is clearly in keeping with modern thought that any necessary financial burden should fall on the shoulders of the whole community. It is suggested that the fairest and most efficient method of providing this finance is by way of Treasury grant out of central taxation.

[1] Cmd. 5435, para. 85.

CHAPTER XIV

ORGANIZATION

The principal services that are essential in any legal aid scheme are competent legal advice and legal representation in any case where this is necessary. If funds are made available there will be no difficulty in providing these services but there are a number of alternative methods of organizing the work. We have argued [1] that persons receiving legal assistance without any cost to themselves should be catered for entirely by legal aid centres unless they prefer to consult a private firm, and that all other assisted persons should be referred to private firms of solicitors who would receive payment from the controlling body. It only remains to consider which would be the most suitable body to control the scheme.

At present the Poor Persons' Procedure is controlled entirely by the Poor Persons' Committees of the Law Societies, the appointments to the committees being nominally confirmed by the Lord Chancellor ; the administration expenses are paid by the Treasury but there does not appear to have been any attempt by the Government to exercise control. The criminal provisions are under the Home Office ; in these cases the courts make the grants of certificates, and the expense of the defence of poor prisoners is borne by local funds. Legal advice and representation in any other courts are provided in miscellaneous ways, including numerous private social service organizations supported by charitable, and in some cases public, funds.

We have stressed throughout the importance of dealing with the problem of legal aid as a whole. Everybody who has gone deeply into the problem has been convinced that organization of an efficient scheme is difficult and can only be successfully accomplished if the matter is looked at from all angles and, in particular, if legal assistance in litigation is not divorced from legal advice. Failure to appreciate this is largely responsible for the failure of the various committees to deal with High Court litigation by poor persons ; the Lawrence Committees were concerned only with litigation in the High Court and the Finlay Committee only with the other legal needs of the poor, and the exclusion of one part of the problem from the scope of the

[1] Chap. XII, *supra*.

enquiries was bound to limit their usefulness. From a practical point of view also, advice and negotiation cannot be separated from litigation since it is extremely difficult to define the point at which a case should be handed over by the advice organization to the organization for giving assistance in litigation, and we have already suggested that some cases should be dealt with throughout by the legal aid centres and others by private firms. If this was not accepted and it was decided that these two functions should be carried out in different ways it would still be important that there should be one overall control, because there would be a constant interchange between advice department and litigation department and only by making one body responsible for both would friction and loss of efficiency be avoided. Also a body is needed, with close contact with both aspects of the work which can provide the necessary leadership to make legal aid as a whole into a thorough and complete service to the community, with such degree of uniformity throughout the country as is desirable.

There are four existing bodies to whom the work might be entrusted: a Government department, local authorities, the Law Societies and the Poor Man's Lawyer organizations. Alternatively a new organization might be set up for the purpose.

Some consideration has already been given to the difficulties which would arise from giving control to a Government department. The independence of the legal profession is a valuable protection for the individual against encroachments on his liberty by the State. The matters on which he requires professional assistance frequently arise from the actions of the State, which is directly involved in such topics as pensions, income tax and employment, and indirectly in many other questions. A Government legal aid department would therefore often be in conflict with another Government department and the public could have little confidence in its impartiality.

Dr. Cohn's conclusion is that legal advice bureaux should be run by the local authorities and the advantages which are urged in favour of this course are: [1]

" Finance—the most urgent question of all legal aid work—flows more freely to public bureaux. Such bureaux are less hampered through the regard which has to be paid to the financial interests of the professions. Above all they have better means

[1] 59 *L.Q.R.*, 262.

to become known to the masses of the population which they have to serve."

Freedom from professional bias is undoubtedly a great advantage but the other two points, it is submitted, do not depend upon public, as opposed to private, control, but upon whether the bureaux are supplied with public or only charitable funds. It is owing to lack of money to provide advice for all who need it that Poor Man's Lawyers, and their equivalents in America, have refrained from encouraging people to apply to them; there would be no difficulty in a bureau under any management becoming known if it wished to increase its clientèle. The assumption that finance and control always go together is false, as is shown by the example of poor persons' procedure, which is financed by public funds but administered by the Law Societies, and by the examples given in the previous chapter.

The arguments against municipal legal advice bureaux are very strong. It has not been suggested that local authorities should have anything to do with assistance in litigation and they could hardly be considered fitted for this purpose. That means a perpetuation of the separation between advice and aid. In fact it is not clear from the Haldane Society's new proposals whether there is to be any body in control of the scheme for aid in litigation at all. There would be advice bureaux run by a large number of separate local authorities; the High Court, each District Registry, each County Court and Police Court would have a legal aid department for granting certificates; representation would be provided by solicitors from the various Rolls of Solicitors kept by each legal aid department and by counsel appointed to act by the Lord Chancellor. Clearly there would not be the close contact between legal advice and further assistance which is desirable, and there would be a multitude of different methods of procedure.

It has, moreover, been repeatedly stated that legal aid is an integral part of the administration of justice and this is no function for local authorities. It does happen that ratepayers provide the funds for the defence of poor prisoners and, if this is considered a wise principle, there is no reason why they should not contribute to the cost of local legal aid bureaux but, with very few exceptions, they have had no experience of administering legal aid, and their reluctance to use their powers to take legal proceedings under the Rent Acts, for example, in spite of pressure from the Ministry of Health, suggests that they do not welcome the addition of this type of work to their many duties. It is thought that solicitors would regard municipal bureaux with disfavour and that the co-operation of the profession would be difficult to obtain. A final, and more serious objection, is that legal aid work would be subject to the influence of party politics on the council. No doubt this is not such a problem here as in America, where it resulted in the closing of several bureaux,[1] but it is easy to see that it would give rise to trouble where local interests were concerned.

Mr. Mervyn Jones, in the report which he prepared before the war, proposed [2] that Poor Man's Lawyer Centres should be developed by means of a Government subsidy and that higher standards and greater uniformity should be obtained by imposing conditions on the grant of a subsidy. There is much to be said in favour of this proposal. Existing centres have had practical experience of the work and many of them have earned the respect of the legal profession, with which they are, in some cases, closely connected, but Dr. Cohn's criticism [3] can be confirmed, that there is a tendency for such organizations to be governed by small groups of irresponsible individuals. If they were to carry out adequately the functions which should be required of the centres, and be entrusted with funds for the purpose, their management would have to be strengthened and linked with some central organization. This suggestion might be incorporated in the further proposal which we are about to discuss.

There are obvious and great advantages in giving control of the legal aid scheme to the Law Societies. In fact there is only one serious objection to this course—the conflict with professional interests, or what are thought to be professional interests. It is only too clear that in the past the legal profession has, for mixed motives, wanted to keep legal aid a matter of charity, and that, because it could not provide sufficient charity it has blinded itself and others to the need that existed. This has not only occurred in this country. Mr. R. H. Smith writes [4] : " From the experience afforded the bar association type [of bureau] is found wanting. Apparently the bar associations thus far have not had a proper vision of the opportunity and they have proved a weak instrument to which to entrust this important

[1] R. H. Smith : *Justice and the Poor.*
[2] *Free Legal Advice in England and Wales*, p. 57.
[3] 59 *L.Q.R.*, 262, note.
[4] *Justice and the Poor.*

service." Dr. Cohn has worked out [1] that the percentage of the population covered who consult municipal bureaux is 150 per cent. higher than in the case of bar association bureaux. The difference is probably one of organization rather than of inherent incapability. If the Law Societies do not welcome the responsibility of providing a comprehensive service of legal aid, a special body should be constituted for the purpose, but the considerations which have led them to oppose any progress up to the present will no longer apply if the principle is once recognized that it is no longer charity which is demanded but public service on reasonable terms.

To guard against excessive concern for professional interests and because the problem is not merely a legal, but also a social, one, the controlling organization should not, in any event, be composed entirely of laywers. This is not a novel suggestion. The 1925 Report [2] suggested that Poor Persons' Committees should have power to co-opt two or three persons representative of charitable or social welfare organizations. The proposal was not specifically embodied in the Rules but some committees did find it a convenient practice. Gurney Champion and Mr. R. H. Smith were both in favour of control being in the hands of lawyers and other elements, and the Haldane Society proposes that the staff of the bureaux should include a social worker. Social service experience is frequently needed in the work and so far as advice centres are concerned the part which social service agencies have played in such schemes as those at Liverpool and Newcastle-upon-Tyne and in numerous smaller schemes makes it foolish and inequitable to exclude them. Those who have worked with the social service organizations know that they have a great deal to contribute to the success of a scheme and that they will help to save it from excessive legalism as well as acting as a safeguard against professional bias.

We are now in a position to give a picture of the organization and working of a legal aid scheme. The scheme described is not put forward dogmatically as the only scheme that will meet the situation but as a demonstration of the practical results of the discussion that has gone before.

There would be a Central Legal Aid Department under the control of a committee appointed by the Law Society, Bar Council and National Council of Social Service jointly. It is suggested that the Law Society should appoint half the members

[1] 59 *L.Q.R.*, 263. [2] Cmd. 2358.

of this committee and the Bar Council and National Council of Social Service should each appoint one quarter ; * the Government might insist on a representative of the Lord Chancellor's Department or the Treasury being on the Committee.

The Central Department would administer funds provided by the Treasury to cover the net cost of the legal aid scheme and would control the organization of the scheme throughout the country. It would not be a Government Department, any more than the Citizens' Advice Bureaux Committee of the National Council of Social Service is a Government Department. It would be responsible to the Government only to the extent of submitting accounts showing that its funds have been administered in accordance with the legislation on legal aid.

Under the Central Department there would be Legal Aid Departments, with similarly constituted committees, for the various parts of the country, possibly one for each district covered by the larger provincial law societies. The local departments would be responsible for the running of an adequate number of Legal Aid Centres in their area, for organizing and supervising the rotas of barristers and solicitors, and the conduct of cases, and for distributing the funds allotted to them by the Central Department. They would also control the local branch of the extended Services Divorce Department, which would have the task of conducting High Court litigation.[1] Existing Poor Man's Lawyer organizations would be able to give valuable assistance to the Local Departments ; their members would be well qualified to serve on the committees or staff of the Departments and their centres would in many cases be the obvious sites for the new Legal Aid Centres.

One other matter of organization requires attention—the question of the authority to grant legal aid certificates. This has been discussed and the desirability of judicial control of this function has been emphasized.[2] It is thought that such control would best be secured by the appointment of a special Registrar or Master to deal with applications for legal aid in all the courts in the district covered by a Local Legal Aid Department. As an alternative the committee of the Local Department could itself

* The Haldane Society in *The Law and Reconstruction* proposed that the Public Legal Service Department—the equivalent of my Central Legal Aid Department—should consist of 11 members—3 appointed by the Law Society, 3 by the Bar Council and 5 by other public bodies. I consider that the Law Society should have a greater share than this.

[1] p. 115, *supra*.

[2] Chap. VII, *supra*.

adjudicate on applications made to it through the centres or otherwise, but if this power was to reside in the committee there can be no doubt that an appeal should lie to the court against the refusal of a certificate. The body with the power to grant or refuse certificates, however constituted, is here described as the certifying authority.

Let us see how this machinery would work in an imaginary case.

A poor person who has met with an accident goes to a Legal Aid Centre. He is interviewed by a clerk and a note is made of his name and address, of his normal income [1] and the nature of the case. As he is not completely destitue he is required to pay a fee of 1*s.* or 2*s.* 6*d.* for advice.[2] He is then interviewed by a solicitor, fuller details of the case are ascertained and it is decided that the matter should be taken up with the insurance company concerned. The applicant is told to send a certificate from the Inspector of Taxes which will show whether it is a case to be handled by the centre.[3] This proves to be the case and negotiations are commenced, but a satisfactory settlement cannot be reached so the applicant is instructed to apply to the certifying authority [4] for a certificate for legal aid in the appropriate proceedings and a statement of the position is submitted by the centre, together with the certificate of the Inspector of Taxes. The certifying authority informs the opposing party that he may appear to show reason why the certificate should not be granted.[5] The opposing party appears and claims that an adequate offer has been made but it is held that this is not a question for the certifying authority to decide and a certificate granting full legal aid is forwarded to the Legal Aid Centre, the case being one for the County Court. The centre handles the case in the same way as an ordinary solicitor's office, if necessary instructing outside counsel from a list of counsel who are prepared to accept briefs on terms laid down for these cases by the Bar Council.[6] A High Court case would proceed in exactly the same way except that not all the Legal Aid Centres would be equipped for High Court litigation and this work would be done either by the Local Department itself or by a selected centre.[7]

If the case is won and costs are recovered from the opponent,

[1] p. 72, *supra*, as to the means enquiry for advice.
[2] p. 127, *supra*, as to charging for advice.
[3] p. 72, *supra*.
[4] Discussed in Chap. VII, *supra*.
[5] pp. 65–7, *supra*.
[6] pp. 116 and 119.
[7] p. 115 and p. 137, *supra*.

these are remitted, with a report of the case to the Local Legal Aid Department. Whether the case is won or lost the Local Department pays the out-of-pocket expenses, in so far as the assisted person cannot afford to pay them, and the Counsel's fees.

So far as advice is concerned any person who is within the legal aid scheme is entitled to one interview at the Legal Advice Centre [1] on payment of the maximum fee, or, if his income justifies it, a reduced fee. If, however, he wishes to be advised by a private firm of solicitors he may either go direct to a solicitor of his own choosing,[2] who is then entitled to charge full fees, or he may ask the centre to give him an introduction to an appropriate solicitor on the rota and this solicitor is only entitled to make the same charge as the centre.

If the matter cannot be disposed of at a single interview any person wishing to take advantage of the legal aid provisions must apply to the certifying authority for full or partial legal aid.[3] The necessary forms and instructions for this purpose are given to him and the certifying authority applies to the centre or the solicitor if it needs further information in order to make a decision.

When a certificate for partial legal aid is given the case is conducted by a private firm of solicitors,[4] the firm being chosen either by the Local Department from the rota of conducting solicitors or by the applicant himself. In the latter case the solicitor is obliged to accept the conditions laid down for firms on the rota. When the certificate is for full legal aid the case is normally conducted by the centre in the manner outlined above, but the applicant is entitled to elect to be represented by a private firm.[5]

Cases conducted by firms of solicitors proceed in the ordinary way except that the solicitors may apply to the Local Department if a grant for out-of-pocket expenses is justified and must obtain the consent of the Local Department to a settlement of the case and report the result of a case on conclusion. If the case is lost the solicitors apply to the Local Department for the fees which are allowed in these cases; if the case is won or settled and costs are recovered from the opposing party these are retained by the solicitors.

All payments by applicants, with the exception of fees for

[1] pp. 107–10, p. 119, *supra*.
[2] p. 115, *supra*.
[3] Chap. VII, *supra*.
[4] p. 117, *supra*.
[5] p. 115, *supra*.

advice, are made to the Local Department. At the conclusion of a case which has been conducted by a firm of solicitors the solicitors submit their bill to the Local Department together with an account of any costs which they have recovered and receive from the Department the balance of costs (if any) which is due to them under the scheme. All costs recovered by centres in cases conducted by them and all fees for advice at centres are handed over to the Local Department. The Local Department requires funds for the maintenance of centres, payment of out-of-pocket expenses, and solicitors' and counsels' fees. These are derived from any money received by the centres and the contributions from persons entitled to partial legal aid and the balance is paid out of the Treasury grant held by the Central Legal Aid Department.

There are no doubt many points on which the above procedure can be criticized and much of it could be deal with in a different way without reducing the assistance given. The fundamental requirement of legal aid reform is to recognize the essential needs of the people concerned—adequate advice and negotiation, representation, remission of court fees and assistance with expenses—there are other, and there may be better, ways in which this could be done and it is only hoped that the material which has been presented may help towards the attainment of the most satisfactory solution.

CHAPTER XV

CONCLUSION

Legal reform in matters of any kind is notoriously slow but when every allowance for this has been made the need for improved legal aid is long overdue and the general lines which it should take are exceptionally clear.

The indifference of the public to this matter and the reasons for it were described in the Introduction to this book but there are many signs that apathy is giving way to concern. Legal aid centres are receiving requests for help from local members of parliament, from the Mayor's Parlour, from the courts and many other quarters, and the problem of providing better facilities is receiving increasing attention. The Law Journal, to quote only one instance has recently written : [1]

> It is, or should be, generally realised that the present system of legal assistance to poor persons is altogether too limited—particularly with regard to the class of persons who can benefit by it—to do more than touch the fringe of the problem created by the fact that litigation is an expensive matter for the litigant. The whole matter is one as to which something will before very long have to be done.

Once it is recognized that large numbers of people cannot use the courts because they are too poor, it is impossible to deny that the provision of legal aid is an essential part of the administration of justice. Denial of justice through poverty is utterly inconsistent with our present conception of democracy and if it is not brought to an end by legal aid the only result will be to accentuate the present tendency to avoid normal legal procedure altogether. It is significant that Sir William Beveridge's survey of the Workmen's Compensation Acts leads him to propose not only a different system for dealing with compensation for workmen's accidents, but to call for an investigation into the possibility of abolishing many, if not all, actions for negligence.[2]

During the writing of this book a committee has been appointed[3] by the Lord Chancellor which, for the first time, is authorized to enquire into the whole subject of legal aid. The opportunity is one which will not occur again for many years. If wise foundations are laid it is possible that from them will

[1] 94 *L.J.*, 42 (5th February, 1944). [2] Cmd. 6404, paras. 258–64.
[3] Announced in the daily papers of 27th May, 1944.

spring a state of affairs in which reasonable litigation will no longer by an impossibility for any man or a foolish luxury for all but the wealthy. " In this light," writes Mr. R. H. Smith,[1] " legal aid work ceases to be an end in itself, it becomes merged in a great design according to which the whole administration of justice is to be rebuilt and reshaped to the end that denial of justice, so far as we now understand it, may cease ".

To guarantee justice for all its citizens is one of the fundamental duties of the State and it has indeed been the folly of the legislator to imagine that this can be done by the charitable efforts of a small section of the community. A new attitude to the problem is required and no amount of patching of an outworn system will meet the case. The expense involved in making justice a reality to all citizens is but a fraction of the money spent on social services and the object to be attained is worthy to take its place among the first principles of the post-war world.

[1] *Justice and the Poor.*

APPENDIX A

PARTICULARS OF LEGAL AID IN TOWNS WITH OVER 100,000 POPULATION

It is the opinion of the American National Association of Legal Aid Organizations, that every town with a population of over 100,000 requires a Legal Aid office with full time staff.[1] That is borne out by the estimate in the 1941 Report of the American Bar Association that a properly run office should expect to advise every year at least one person for every hundred in the population, so that there would be at least 1,000 applicants to be dealt with every year. In actual fact some of the American offices advise each year three or four people for every hundred of the population and this is also the case in Sweden and Denmark, so that it is obvious that in towns of very much less than 100,000 a legal aid office would be justified.

This figure has, however, been selected for the purpose of a survey of the legal aid facilities that exist in large towns in order to keep the report within reasonable proportions. Most of the towns have considerably over 100,000 population, some of them millions, and in relation to population the numbers dealt with by most of the Poor Man's Lawyer organizations are fantastically low. It must be remembered that some of the schemes, for example Liverpool, Manchester and Salford, and Newcastle-upon-Tyne, cover several towns and urban districts, each of which individually has more than 100,000 population, so that collectively their population is very much greater than would appear at first sight. Similarly there are many towns which are individually below this population figure but which form a group containing well over 100,000 people. These are not included in the report.

Some of the smaller towns have better schemes than those mentioned, and deal with more applicants than towns many times their size. At Chesterfield, for example, (population 64,160) 174 applicants were advised in 1943 as compared with 35 or 40 at Wolverhampton (population 133,212) but on the whole the smaller towns have correspondingly less facilities and in many cases nothing which could properly be called a legal aid scheme at all.

It would, of course, not be fair to judge the various organizations on the work which they are doing at the moment under war-time conditions, and a description is given of peace-time activities as far as possible. At the same time the decline which has taken place in most instances shows how unstable are the foundations of most of the schemes. This is inevitable having regard to the charitable and voluntary nature of the activities but it is particularly unfortunate because the need is greater now than it has ever been before—so much greater that the Services have had to innovate schemes in the interests of morale.

---

[1] R. H. Smith and Bradway, op. cit., Chap. XV.

In the following notes no mention is made as a rule of Poor Persons' Procedure in the High Court or of assistance given to serving men under the Services Legal Aid Schemes. The scheme drawn up by the Law Society for legal aid in connection with Citizens' Advice Bureaux is described as the " C.A.B. Scheme ".

Birmingham.—The Birmingham Poor Man's Lawyer Association was formed in 1908. There was a steady increase in the numbers from 422 in 1909 to 4,328 in 1938, when there were about fifty lawyers in the Association, including the Clerk to the Magistrates, and the Town Clerk was the Honorary Secretary. There is very close contact with the Birmingham Law Society, whose staff and premises are used by the Association, and the Rules provide that four members of the Committee shall be elected by the Law Society and that the Chairman and Honorary Secretary shall, if possible, be members of the Committee of the Law Society. Before the war there were four separate Centres and another was about to be opened.

The organization has suffered considerably during the war. No records have been kept but it is estimated that about 3,500 interviews have been given each year. There are about twenty-two solicitors who take turns in advising at the two Centres which remain open. One lawyer attends on Saturday afternoons at the Birmingham Settlement and six or eight at the Central Hall between 2 p.m. and 6 p.m. on a week day. At the latter between 50 and 100 interviews are given each week and there is not sufficient time to deal with the cases adequately. There is no clerical assistance; the adviser ascertains applicants' means, no definite means test being applied, and fills in the Case Sheets. The Centre is not supplied with adequate reference books and no letters are written.

Cases requiring representation in the High Court are, of course, referred to the Poor Persons' Committee and are subject to long delays. There are about 20 solicitors who have volunteered to take County Court cases on the basis that they will make no charge to their clients but will retain any costs recovered from the opposing party. It is found that this arrangement is really only effective in Workmen's Compensation cases. The Citizens' Society sometimes assists applicants to pay out-of-pocket expenses. No representation is provided for Police Court cases.

The expenses of the Association, £20 or £30 a year, are subscribed by solicitors.

Blackburn.—Apart from Poor Persons' Procedure there is no assistance other than that given by one firm of solicitors who do what they can for applicants referred to them by the Citizens' Advice Bureau.

Blackpool.—The Law Society has a list of solicitors who will assist persons referred by the C.A.B. on such terms as they think fit.

Bolton.—The Honorary Solicitors of the Bolton Guild of Help assist with about 12 cases per annum but do not act in court cases.

Cases requiring court action are sent to another firm and in one recent case the Guild of Help made a grant of £20.

Bournemouth.—No information obtainable.

Bradford.—No information obtainable.

Brighton.—There is a scheme organized by the Sussex Law Society covering Brighton, Hove, Portslade, Rottingdean and Patcham. Before the war 20 solicitors took part, now there are about 6 ; the Social Service Centre ascertains the applicants' means.

Advice is given at solicitors' offices except at Brighton where a P.M.L. sits one night a week. Occasionally cases are investigated and letters written. No representation is provided.

The numbers increased to 495 in the first year of war and have since gone down to 182 per annum. This is apparently not due to evacuation, since the figures for general advice given by the C.A.B. have increased, but to a strict attitude as to means (although the limit is not fixed) and to the advice given under the Services Advice Schemes.

Bristol.—Advice in six-sevenths of the legal cases, which are mostly Landlord and Tenant, Workmen's Compensation and Matrimonial cases, is given by the Secretary of the C.A.B., who is not a qualified lawyer. The remaining cases (130 in 1943) are referred to the offices of one of the 23 solicitors who have placed their names on a rota for giving advice or are dealt with by the Secretary after a discussion on the telephone with one of the solicitors. The solicitors will write letters and sometimes go to great trouble to negotiate a settlement but do not usually obtain police or medical reports or other evidence.

No representation is obtainable in the County Court ; there is a charitable society which sometimes pays the fees to enable matrimonial cases to be represented. There are no funds available for the payment of out-of-pocket expenses.

Cardiff.—No scheme.

Coventry.—No scheme.

Croydon.—There is a P.M.L. Association formerly composed of 20 solicitors and now working under great difficulties with only 2.

Derby.—No information obtainable.

Huddersfield.—No information obtainable.

Hull.—There is a P.M.L. Association run jointly by the Law Society and the Social Service organization. The income test applied is extremely low, £1 10*s.* for a single man, £2 joint income for a married couple, £3 for a married couple with children, and the numbers are extremely low—about 87 per annum.

Representation is provided free to the client. If costs are recovered from the opposing party the solicitors retain two-thirds and the remaining third goes to the Association's funds.

Leeds.—There has been a P.M.L. in Leeds since 1919 ; in 1939 there were 1,330 applications ; it was closed early in the war until May 1941 and since it was re-opened there have been 300–400 applicants each year. It is open from 6.30 to 7.30 p.m. and applicants are said to come from Wakefield, Harrogate and even Bradford and Halifax.

Two lawyers attend together. No letters are written and cases requiring representation are referred to three or four solicitors who are willing to adjust their fees to the client's pocket. There is a Cases Fund for providing out-of-pocket expenses and the organization on one occasion took the unusual step of providing free representation in a High Court case in which a Poor Persons' Certificate was not obtained.

The C.A.B. uses this P.M.L. but sometimes finds it more convenient to send applicants to the offices of a solicitor who can interview them in business hours or to the Poor Persons' Committee or to get advice from the bureau's Honorary solicitors.

Leicester.—The P.M.L. Association at Leicester is now operating the C.A.B. scheme. The P.M.L. sits fortnightly and the number of interviews has dropped from 699 in 1938 to 272 in 1942. 164 of the cases were referred to the Rota for further action.

Liverpool.—There is a P.M.L. Association run by the Law Society in close co-operation with the Personal Service Society, which also assists the Law Society in connection with applications to the Poor Persons' Committee. It covers a wide and heavily populated area. There is a centre at Liverpool open three afternoons a week, one at Seacombe, open fortnightly, and normally another at Birkenhead but at the present time solicitors are advising at their private offices. Crosby and Waterloo are within the area but are not adequately covered by the present scheme.

The number of applications has risen steadily over a number of years at the rate of about 100 a year and in 1942/3 was 2,262. The means test is practically identical with that applied for free advice in the C.A.B. scheme.

Apart from negotiation in minor matters the assistance is confined to advice. There is no system of free representation or reduced fees apart from some matrimonial and affiliation cases in the Police Court where the Law Society arranges representation for the sum of £1 1*s*. The Law Society contributes to the expenses of the Association.

Manchester and Salford.—Manchester claims to have had the first provincial Poor Man's Lawyer and the P.M.L. Association, which was formed at a later date, is the most effective in the country. As at Liverpool it is very largely controlled by the local Law Society but it has not the same close connection with social service. Until recently it shared the offices of the Poor Persons' Committee but it now has an office of its own and a full-time salaried Assistant Secretary ; with this office the expenses will amount to about £250 per annum which is raised from a variety of sources—the Law Society, charitable bodies, private subscribers, and from a grant made under the Poor Law Act. A report of its work is published annually.

There are branches at Hulme, Salford, Ancoats, Collyhurst and Wythenshaw, where a P.M.L. attends weekly, or in one case, fortnightly. About 15 lawyers, out of the 60 available in peacetime, take part in the advising and the figures for advice are as follows :

1936	1937	1938	1939	1939–40	1940–1	1941–2	1942–3
2,500	3,100	3,965	4,290	3,308	2,805	2,879	3,097

Representation is carried out by firms on a rota, of whom there are about 70 in peacetime. The solicitors retain any fees recovered from the opposing party, and are expected to use their discretion as to the charges made to their clients. A conducting solicitor is obliged by the Rules to report to the Assistant Secretary his reasons for declining any case which has been referred to him and, on request, the outcome of any case which he has taken up. A fund is available for assisting needy litigants with out-of-pocket expenses. There is a special arrangement for Police Court cases whereby one of the solicitors undertakes to take up any cases which require representation in a particular week. The proportion of cases referred to the Poor Persons' Committee and to solicitors can be seen from the following figures for 1942–3.

Total of Applications	Dealt with at Branch	Referred to Solicitors	Referred to P.P.C.
3,097	2,341	510	246

Middlesbrough.—The only legal aid is provided by the Honorary solicitors of the C.A.B.

Newcastle.—For 35 years legal advice has been provided through the social service organization and subsequently through the Law Society. Before the war there were Centres at Newcastle, Gateshead and South Shields but now in Gateshead, as in other heavily populated areas, applicants have to be referred to solicitors' offices. In 1938 there were 198 applicants to the Newcastle centre.

The C.A.B. scheme has now been adopted with slight modifications. In 1943, 157 cases were referred to solicitors, as compared with 98 referred to the Poor Persons' Committee. The P.P.C., which receives many applications from other sources, had 504 cases outstanding.

Norwich.—As a result of approaches made by the C.A.B. to the Law Society a scheme was introduced in September 1943. Appointments are made for applicants at the solicitors' offices and any necessary action is taken, the solicitors only receiving such fees as are obtained from the opposing party.

From September 1943 to March 1944 12 cases were referred to the 20 firms taking part in the scheme. A great many more tenancy problems are dealt with either by the Town Clerk or a Tenants' Defence League.

There is no fixed means test and no fund for out-of-pocket expenses.

Nottingham.—Two lawyers attend at the C.A.B. when required (about once a fortnight) and there are three others who will answer queries over the telephone. Letters are written but no representation provided. Including cases dealt with by telephone about 100 people per annum receive legal advice.

Oldham.—Three lawyers take part in a scheme controlled by the Council of Social Welfare. Advice is given at the solicitors' offices or over the telephone and it is estimated that about 25 applicants are dealt with in a year. Letters are written but no representation is provided. The only means test applied is whether the applicant is able to pay the fees.

Plymouth.—The C.A.B. scheme was adopted by the Law Society but never came into operation.

There is a P.M.L. session weekly from 7–9 p.m. and between 1,000 and 1,100 people are interviewed each year. There were formerly two solicitors who advised but now there is only one. No letters are written or representation provided.

Portsmouth.—No legal assistance other than that given by the C.A.B.'s Honorary Solicitors at their own offices.

Preston.—The C.A.B. sends cases to the Honorary Secretary of the Law Society who has a list of 6 or 7 solicitors who are said to do everything that is necessary.

There is no fund for out-of-pocket expenses.

Reading.—The Council of Social Service has a rota of nine solicitors who will advise applicants at their offices or the C.A.B. over the telephone. The advice is not always given free. Any assistance or representation is left to the discretion of the individual solicitor and the Council of Social Service sometimes provides funds. The income scales of the C.A.B. scheme are applied.

The number of enquiries in 1938 was 39 ; in 1939, 35 ; in 1943, 650, but only 10 of these were referred to solicitors ; in probably 50 more cases the Secretary of the C.A.B. rang up a solicitor before giving the advice.

Rhondda.—No legal aid.

St. Helens.—The C.A.B. arranges for solicitors to advise and, if possible, to take up cases.

Sheffield.—Before the war the Council of Social Service, in co-operation with the Law Society, had a rota of 30 solicitors who attended at three centres. 2,340 applicants were advised in 1938. As a wartime measure appointments are made at solicitors' offices and 338 applicants were given appointments in 1943.

The income test is £2 per week excluding the amount of the rent.

There is difficulty in raising fees for court proceedings, which are found to be necessary in many cases.

Southampton.—Formerly there was a P.M.L. centre but now the C.A.B. refers anyone needing legal advice to the offices of solicitors who charge what they think fit.

Southend.—Solicitors formerly attended at the offices of the Guild of Social Service but now there are 11 solicitors who advise at their offices. Sometimes letters are written but no representation is provided.

Recent figures for advice are as follows :

1937–8	1938–9	1939–40	1940–1	1941–2	1942–3
315	247	101	81	54	26

The virtual extinction of legal advice is no doubt partly due to evacuation and the increase of wages but the number of general enquiries to the C.A.B. in 1942–3 was 2,799.

Stockport.—No information obtainable.

Stoke-on-Trent.—Enquiries to the C.A.B. are allocated to firms of solicitors. Workmen's Compensation cases are sometimes represented but otherwise there is no representation and hardship arises particularly in matrimonial cases in the Police Court.

Sunderland.—There is no co-ordinated scheme. The C.A.B. gives legal advice after consulting a solicitor or refers the applicant to his office; 46 cases were dealt with in this way in 1943. The Law Society has a list of 15 solicitors who sometimes provide representation in compensation cases, receiving fees only from the opposing party. The Clerk to the Magistrates gives preliminary advice on civil Police Court cases which are not pending in the Court; these amounted to about 100 in 1943; and the local Bar also assists with matrimonial and affiliation cases in the Police Court. There is no fund for out-of-pocket expenses.

Swansea.—There is one solicitor who will advise the C.A.B. over the telephone, but if an interview is needed a charge is usually made. A P.M.L. is sadly needed.

Walsall.—The Civic Guild of Help depends upon its two Honorary Solicitors and sometimes assists by paying court or other fees.

Wolverhampton.—The C.A.B. scheme has been adopted with a much stricter means qualification. To get free assistance the income of a married couple's household, after deduction of rent, must not exceed £2 a week plus 5*s.* for each child of school age, and their readily realizable assets must not be worth more than £40.

There is no P.M.L. centre and in 1943 between 35 and 40 applicants were advised. The scheme deals only with personal and domestic troubles arising out of the war.

York.—Before the war a P.M.L. used to sit fortnightly and 65 cases were dealt with in the year 1937/8. Now the C.A.B. scheme has been adopted but there is no charge for advice and the means test for free aid is £2 for a single person, and £3 for two persons, with an allowance of 10*s.* for each dependant. One lawyer attends weekly at the offices of the Community Council to give advice and there were 205 applicants in 1942/3.

Representation is provided by the nine firms on the panel, charging according to means.

LONDON

Only a few examples of Poor Man's Lawyer Centres in London can be given. First of all two centres which are typical of centres affiliated to the Bentham Committee.

Kensington.—One lawyer attends one evening a week, with a clerk. No action is taken beyond advising and drafting letters for the applicant to write. Cases which require representation are sometimes referred to the Bentham Committee. No records are kept.

Alford House, Lambeth.—This centre was in operation for many years before the war, advice being given on one night a week, when about four lawyers attended. Before the war about 250 cases were dealt with each year; in the first year of the war about 100 cases were dealt with and at the end of 1940 the centre was closed. It was re-opened by one of the lawyers in 1942 and in the first year about 50 cases were dealt with. The lawyer undertakes negotiations in cases but no representation.

Toynbee Hall is also affiiliated to the Bentham Committee but, until the war, paid a firm of solicitors to undertake the representation of court cases. Advice was given on one night a week, when there was an average attendance of four or five lawyers; during the war one or two lawyers attend. There is no clerical assistance, no records are kept and action beyond advice is seldom taken. About 1,600 clients were advised in 1938 now 20 to 25 are interviewed weekly.

University House is a centre which opened during the first air raids on London when the Poor Man's Lawyer ceased to attend at Oxford House and St. Margaret's House. A K.C. gave the Settlement £100 for a solicitor to be employed to represent people who had been admitted to the Rest Centre and who were found to be paying rent for demolished houses. The Solicitor continued to give his services free when the donation was exhausted and built up the bureau. Eight lawyers attend three times a week: on Wednesday from 2 p.m. to 9 p.m., Saturdays 2.30 p.m. to 4.30 p.m., and Sundays 10.30 a.m. to 1 p.m.; during the rest of the week a clerk takes particulars from applicants who call and makes appointments. Pressure on the lawyers is heavy and about half the cases are taken away by them for further consideration. All applicants are first interviewed by the clerk and records are made. The bureau received a gift of £20 worth of books and takes regularly a legal journal, the County Court Reports, and Citizens' Advice Notes. From 1941 to 1943 the number of applications were 151, 250, 500, 800. No fixed income test is applied; the matter is left to the adviser's discretion.

Any necessary action whether in or out of court and including criminal and High Court proceedings is taken, the advisers themserves guaranteeing payment. Costs recovered are paid to a fund for administration expenses.

Mary Ward Settlement.—This centre was opened in August 1942 to assist C.A.B.'s north of the Thames. It has a full-time Registrar and full-time secretary-typist, two solicitors who attend three or four days a week, and a small amount of additional help from others. In the year 1942–3 it gave 3,646 interviews (2,069 cases), wrote 3,865 letters and dealt with 1,360 telephone enquiries. Detailed records are kept and the centre has the loan of a valuable library. At a preliminary interview the means of the applicant are ascertained and advice is not given if the income exceeds £3 10*s.* in the case of single persons, and £4 10*s.* joint income in the case of married couples, plus 10*s.* for each child. Applicants come not only from the central London area but from East Ham, Hammersmith, Staines, High Wycombe, New Barnet, Hertford and places well into Essex. Publicity is not given to the centre because it would not be able to cope with the influx of cases, which already come from many sources in addition to C.A.B.'s.

Extensive negotiations are undertaken but representation is a serious difficulty. The centre is now affiliated to the Bentham Committee but only a limited number of cases can be referred to that organization ; the remainder are referred to one of twenty firms who have agreed to give assistance, and to show consideration for the applicants' slender means. It is stated that in clear claims, such help is generally obtained without difficulty, but in cases of any doubt, or where there is obviously no money to be obtained as a result of litigation, or in the case of matrimonial proceedings in the Police Court, representation is by no means easily obtained. Many people who have been referred to solicitors do not go to the solicitor and this is put down to the fear of " getting into a solicitor's hands ". It is found that magistrates do not consider applications for legal aid certificates sufficiently sympathetically and on occasions a solicitor at the centre has briefed counsel in criminal matters to save the applicant from having to pay a solicitor's costs in addition to counsel's fees.

The present annual cost of the centre is about £455.

Society of Our Lady of Good Counsel.—This is a Catholic society which assists any person who has not more than £2 per week or £50 capital. The society aims at amicable settlement of disputes but occasionally advances funds for Police and County Court cases. It has a number of Honorary Counsel for opinions and the work is divided into fourteen different categories so that solicitors and barristers may volunteer for work for which they are particularly suited. Before the war it was dealing with upwards of a thousand cases per annum, there was an honorary secretary with paid clerical staff and the expenses came to over £700 per annum. No information is available with regard to its wartime activities.

Women's and Children's Protection Society.—This is not a Poor Man's Lawyer but does assist poor women and children with regard to proceedings in matrimonial, affiliation, and guardianship matters. In 1938 813 applications were received and its expenditure was £1,137.

APPENDIX B

COMPARATIVE SUMMARY OF LEGAL AID PROVISIONS

The analysis which follows is based largely on reports [1] made to the League of Nations in 1924 and 1925 and in the case of some countries it has not been possible to bring the information up to date or to ascertain the practice on certain points. The statements should not, therefore, particularly in this simplified form, be regarded as absolutely accurate or comprehensive but merely as a general estimate of the position outside this country. Unless otherwise stated the observations do not apply to provisions for legal aid in criminal matters.

1. Countries where there is no Legal Aid

China.—This country's report, dated 1925, recognized the need for legal aid and declared the Government's intention of setting up a special institution for the purpose. The Chinese Embassy is unaware of any provisions having been made.

Cuba.—There are provisions but they are ineffective because the Government does not maintain any body of advocates to render the prescribed services.

Canada.—In British Columbia there is none ; in other provinces it is extremely limited.

India.—British India had no legal aid at the time of the League Report and the India Office has no information of any developments.

Panama.

Note : In addition to the above, legal aid is so restricted as to be virtually non-existent in the following States :

Canada.—The provinces other than British Columbia have only the old English *in forma pauperis* procedure and in some cases no representation is provided.

Ireland.—*In forma pauperis* procedure in the High Court only, limited to persons not worth £25. Remission of court fees in the District Court.

New Zealand.—Only *in forma pauperis* procedure.*

Northern Ireland.—There is only *in forma pauperis* procedure, but new Rules are about to be introduced and there is charitable assistance in the lower courts.

2. Countries having some Organization providing Legal Advice

Legal advice in litigious matters is usually provided by the organization which deals with applications for legal aid. In the following countries there are organizations for the specific purpose of giving advice, although they may give aid in litigation as well :

[1] Published by the League of Nations as *Legal Aid for the Poor* (V. Legal, 1927, V. 27.)

* Legislation has been passed to introduce a system similar to the present English Poor Persons' Procedure, but it is not yet in operation—Poor Persons' Legal Aid Act, 1939.

Argentine.—The Labour Department runs an Advice Bureau for workers. At Buenos Aires the College of Advocates provides advice.
Australia.—Queensland : The Department of Justice.
Austria.—Municipal bureaux at Vienna, Linz and Innsbruck.
Belgium.—Each bar must provide a legal consultation bureau.
Brazil.—The Legal Aid Commissions and private institutions.
Czechoslovakia.—Trade Unions and charitable organizations.
Danzig.—A municipal bureau.
Denmark.—The Danish Student's Association.
England and Wales.—Miscellaneous charitable organizations.
Estonia.
Finland.—Municipal bureaux in seven towns.
France.—Private bureaux of the Order of Advocates.
Germany.—Some municipal and some private bureaux.
Hungary.—The Public Charity Department at Budapest ; also Trade Unions and provincial Orders of Advocates.
Italy.—The public Legal Aid Office and private organizations.
Japan.—Some police stations and private organizations.
Latvia.—The Council of Advocates, Trade Unions and Associations of Tenants.
Monaco.—The Procurator General, presiding over a Legal Aid Bureau.
Netherlands.—The Legal Aid Bureaux attached to the courts, and private organizations.
Northern Ireland.—The Belfast Legal Dispensary.
Norway.—Official bureaux in four towns.
Peru.
Poland.—Municipal bureaux ; also Councils of Advocates, Trade Unions and other bodies.
Roumania.—Councils of Advocates.
Scotland.—Private organizations in Edinburgh and Glasgow.
South Africa.—Johannesburg Free Legal Advice Bureau.
Sweden.—Municipal bureaux.
Switzerland.—Public offices in some Cantons. At Basle the President of the Civil Court gives consultations weekly.
U.S.A.—Some municipal and some private bureaux.

3. Means

A. Countries where Poverty need not be shown

In every country a poverty test is applied, but in some countries there are certain types of case where legal aid is not limited to poor persons :

Argentine.—" Workers who suffer accidents or their families " are assisted in the courts by the Labour Department Free Legal Aid Service without, apparently, having to show poverty.

In the province of Jujuy " persons under arrest " are to be defended without being required to make a declaration as to means.

Belgium.—Defendants in criminal proceedings.
Danzig.—Advice is given to any person concerning industrial and social legislation.

Denmark.—Where a defendant appears without an advocate in a matrimonial case or in a case in which heirs are claiming possession of a missing person's estate an advocate is appointed to act at the expense of the Treasury.

Estonia.—A defendant in a criminal case is entitled to representation on request and in certain workmen's compensation cases poverty need not be shown.

Latvia.—Workmen's accident cases.

Norway.—In divorce and separation cases the court is to appoint counsel—

1. For the defendant if he does not appear.
2. If one party is represented, for the other party on request.

B. Countries where there is a Fixed Means Test

In the great majority of countries no definite financial qualification is stipulated but the applicant has to show inability to bear the cost of the proceedings. The following are the exceptions :

Australia : New South Wales.—The income requirement is now related to the " needs basic wage " and there is no longer a fixed figure, but there is also a property limit of £100.

Queensland.—Not worth £25 (Supreme Court).

South Australia.—Not worth £100.

Western Australia.—Not worth £50 and not earning the " basic wage " ; but in special circumstances there is no fixed limit.

Victoria.—Property not exceeding £50.

Tasmania.—Not worth £50 or, in special circumstances, £100 and not earning more than £3 or, in special circumstances, £4 a week.

Canada.—The amounts for the different provinces are not stated except for Nova Scotia (not worth $50), but it is likely that there is a fixed limit since the procedure, where it exists, is based on the English *in forma pauperis* procedure.

England and Wales.—£2–£4 a week income and £50–£100 capital assets.

Ireland.—Not worth £25 (High Court).

Northern Ireland.—Not worth £25.

Peru.—Not more than an income of 150 Peruvian pounds per annum.

Salvador.—Not worth more than $200.

South Africa.—Means not exceeding amounts varying from £10 to £25 according to the Province.

Spain.—Extremely involved test. See Chapter VI.

U.S.A.—In Arkansas, not worth $10 (this may well have been raised), in New York $300 (raised from $100 in 1935). In other States the limits are not fixed.

4. The Certifying Authority

By far the most common practice is for the trial court to be the authority for granting legal aid ; it may be assumed that, so far as official schemes are concerned, this is so in all countries other than those which come under one of the following headings. It should be noted that the court is the authority for granting aid even when it delegates its authority to a commission; the only exception to this is Haiti, where the commission is appointed by the Secretary of State for Justice.

A. Countries where the Grant is made by Practising Lawyers *

Australia: Western Australia.
Tasmania.
England and Wales.
Roumania.
San Marino.

B. Countries where the Grant is made by Officials

Australia: New South Wales.—The Public Solicitor.
Queensland.—The grant is made by the Court but the Attorney General has power to remit fees payable to the State.
Denmark and Iceland.—The Minister of Justice; in the courts of first instance the Prefect or Overpraesident.
Finland.—In addition to the power of the courts to grant legal aid there are municipal legal aid bureaux in several towns which have power to decide on applications for representation made to them.
Haiti.—The Secretary of State for Justice on the advice of a commission composed of a Government Commissioner, a magistrate and three advocates.
Monaco.—A legal aid bureau, presided over by the Procurator General attached to the Court of Appeal.
Norway.—The Minister of Justice.
Switzerland.—In some Cantons the Minister of Justice or the communal authority makes the grant, but in most Cantons the Court makes the grant.

C. Countries where there are Legal Aid Commissions

Belgium.—A Judge, appointed for each court for the year and assisted by the Procurator.
Brazil.—The President of the central commission is appointed by the Minister of Justice, other members by the Brazilian Order of Advocates. Auxiliary commissions are appointed by the central commission. The commissions report to the trial judge, who gives the actual decision. In two States there are no Commissions.
Egypt.—A magistrate, a procurator and an advocate for each court.
France.—Similar to Belgium.
Haiti.—See B.
Italy.—A member of the court, a public official and an advocate.
Scotland.—Practising lawyers.
Switzerland.—In some Cantons.

* The Scottish Committee has proposed that formal admission by the Court, as at present, should be abolished, at least in the Sheriff Court. The grant would then be in the hands of practising lawyers appointed by their professional organizations, but it is proposed that there should then be an appeal to the Sheriff-Substitute.

D. Countries where there is No Appeal against the refusal of Legal Aid

In most countries an appeal is allowed, in others the position is not clear. The following are the countries where there is definitely no appeal ; none of them, except England and Tasmania, is a country where practising lawyers decide the applications.

Australia : Tasmania.
Brazil.—There is an appeal, however, in at least two of the States.
England and Wales.
Estonia.
France.—The Procurator, but not the applicant, may appeal.
Haiti.
Scotland.
Sweden.—No appeal if the decision is given by the full Court and not by one Judge alone.

5. Benefits of the Grant

It is virtually universal for a grant of legal aid to involve the provisional remission of court and other judicial fees. It may also be assumed, although not expressly stated in some instances, that an assisted person cannot be required to give security for his opponent's costs.

Two further benefits remain to be considered—the provision of a legal representative and the payment of the assisted person's out-of-pocket expenses.

A. Representation

All countries which have any legal aid at all provide representatives for some cases. In many, however, the representative receives no payment except from an opponent who has been ordered to pay costs. It is extremely difficult to tell whether this is so or not in some of the countries but it is certain or extremely probable that there is remuneration attached to the representatives of poor persons in the following :

Countries where there is Paid Representation of Poor Persons

Argentine.
Australia : New South Wales.—A salaried Public Solicitor.
Queensland.—The Public Curator or lawyers who receive fees.
South Australia.—A salaried Public Solicitor.
Victoria.—A salaried Public Solicitor.
Western Australia.—Lawyers receive reduced fees.
Austria.
Brazil : Alagoas.—A salaried Director of Legal Aid.
Amazonas.
Czechoslovakia.—Fees in certain matters.
Denmark.
Finland.—Municipal bureaux.
Germany.—Lawyers receive reduced fees.
Hungary.

Norway.
South Africa.—In cases where representation is arranged by the Johannesburg Legal Aid Bureau.
Sweden.
Switzerland.—In Federal Courts and at least eight Cantons.
U.S.A.—In some States.

B. Countries where Assistance is given with the Out-of-pocket Expenses of the Action

The expenses which are most commonly provided in the countries listed below are travelling expenses and witnesses' expenses. Where other items are covered in addition, they are specifically mentioned.

Australia: Western Australia.—The representative certifies that the expenses were necessary.

New South Wales.—" Out-of-pockets " may be paid from a fund.

Victoria.—Fees of witnesses, expenses of taking evidence on commission, free copies of documents.

Austria.—All stamp duties and Treasury dues; fees of witnesses and experts, cost of copies of records and documents.
Belgium.—Travelling and subsistence allowances of experts, witnesses and public officers, fees of experts, the cost of publishing legal notices, and other authorized disbursements.
Brazil.—Travelling and subsistence allowances.
Czechoslovakia.—As in Austria; also (in former Hungarian territory) cost of publishing legal notices.
Danzig.—As in Germany.
Denmark and Iceland.—Postal charges, cost of publishing legal notices, travelling expenses, daily allowances and other sums due to witnesses and experts.
Egypt.—Free documents and copies; the necessary expenditure involved in obtaining the opinion of experts and calling witnesses, cost of publishing legal notices.
France.—Fees of experts and payments to authorized witnesses.
Germany.—Witnesses' and experts' allowances, stamp duties and other out-of-pockets.
Greece.—Expenses in general.
Haiti.
Hungary.—Amounts due to witnesses and experts.
Italy.—Documents and copies free, travelling and other expenses of experts, expenses necessarily incurred in obtaining the evidence of witnesses, free legal notices; public officials and experts must provide their services free.
Latvia.—Free legal notices, emoluments of experts, witnesses' allowances.
Luxemburg.—Allowances and subsistence of witnesses, free copies of documents and legal notices.
Monaco.—As in France.
Norway.—Travelling and subsistence allowances.
Peru.—Reduction of stamp duty, free documents.
Poland.—As in Germany.

Sweden.
Switzerland.—In some Cantons costs of experts and witnesses.
Salvador.—Stamp duties.
San Marino.—Stamp duties ; experts and all other persons exercising a liberal profession to give their services free.
U.S.A.—In some States.

6. Liability for Costs

A. The Opponent's Liability for Costs

The general rule is that the opponent's liability for his own and the poor person's costs is the same in a poor person's suit, as in any other, that is to say, he will normally have to pay the poor person's costs if he is unsuccessful and if he is successful he will have to pay his own costs in so far as they cannot be recovered from the poor person. There is a minor concession in Germany, where the opponent is provisionally exempt from payment of fees and expenses, and in Basle, Switzerland, where neither party pays Court fees if the poor person loses the case. The only country which has adopted the English rule that the unsuccessful opponent of a poor person is not normally made liable for the poor person's costs, is Tasmania.

B. The Assisted Person's Liability for his Opponent's Costs

In many States the assisted person is under the normal liability for his opponent's costs ; and there is no case, apart from England, where the assisted person is expressly exempted from this liability, but there are the following special provisions with regard to payment of the costs.

Brazil.—In the Federal Courts an assisted person may be ordered to pay costs but the costs can only be recovered if he acquires sufficient resources to pay them before the action for recovery is barred by lapse of time. There is a similar provision in the State of Rio Grande do Norte.
Egypt.—In the Mehkemehs and the Cantonal Courts recourse may not be had against the dwelling-house of the assisted person.
Luxemburg.—Execution against the assisted person is only allowed if the Court considers that his circumstances have sufficiently improved.
Spain.—The assisted person can only be proceeded against if possessed of sufficient resources.

C. The Assisted Person's Liability for his Own Costs

Generally speaking an assisted person has nothing to pay for the application or the conduct of his side of the case, except out-of-pocket expenses in States where these are not provided. In Italy a fee has to be paid on applying for assistance, and in Spain the applicant has to pay the costs of the application if it is not granted.

In the State of Espirito Santo, Brazil, an assisted person who loses his case ceases to be regarded as a poor person, in the absence of any provision to the contrary, and is required to pay all the expenses, but it is more usual for the assisted person to be liable for the fees and expenses which have been remitted only if he acquires sufficient resources to pay them.

Countries where the Assisted Person may be ordered to pay his Own Costs if he acquires Sufficient Resources

In some States only the acquisition of resources as a result of the action is contemplated, but where this is not specifically mentioned in the particulars given below, the provisions are not limited in this way. Where the assisted person is successful his opponent will, of course, normally pay his costs and his own liability will be confined to any balance of costs due from him or to cases where payment is not forthcoming from the opponent.

Australia : New South Wales.—If more than £50 net recovered.
South Australia.—Out-of-pockets payable if money recovered.
Western Australia.—If more than £50 net recovered.

Belgium.

Brazil : Federal.—Expenses payable, *State of Santo Paulo*, *State of Matto Grosso*: A percentage of winnings payable in addition to the scale fees.

Czechoslovakia.

Egypt.—In the Cantonal Courts, if a claim for more than a certain amount is successful.

England and Wales.—Out of property recovered in the suit.

Estonia.

France.

Germany.

Hungary.—Stamp duties and out-of-pocket expenses may have to be refunded.

Italy.

Japan.

Latvia, *Poland*, *San Marino*, *Spain*: Out of property recovered in the suit.

Sweden.—If resources acquired within five years.

Switzerland.—In the Federal Courts and most Cantons.

APPENDIX C

FIGURES RELATING TO POOR PERSONS' PROCEDURE

1. Applications to London and Provincial Committees *

Year	Applications pending at commencement of year		Applications made during the year		Applications granted during the year	
1918	—		4,411		2,293	
1919	1,454		—		—	
1922	1,202		3,050		1,173	
1923	1,377		2,953		1,280	
1924	1,701		3,223		1,464	
1925	1,795		—		—	
1926	1,599		4,284		2,147	
	London	Provinces	London	Provinces	London	Provinces
1927	133	491	1,540	—	769	—
1928	114	685	1,784	2,719	742	1,358
1929	140	751	1,921	2,896	864	1,451
1930	116	688	1,974	3,114	889	1,569
1931	—	733	2,275	3,331	1,037	1,779
1932	—	716	2,372	3,596	1,048	2,004
1933	—	732	2,531	3,835	1,117	2,114
1934	—	718	2,655	4,074	1,112	2,205
1935	—	790	2,792	3,993	1,116	2,219
1936	—	950	2,690	4,038	1,292	2,279
1937	271	914	2,947	4,503	1,221	2,289
1938	381	1,223	6,737	11,866	2,873	5,611
1939	928	2,954	3,833	6,723	1,965	3,795
1940	520	2,760	3,161	5,501	1,068	2,314
1941	973	3,301	3,849	6,052	1,245	2,294
1942	1,605	3,448	7,507	5,520	2,623	2,280
1943	4,407	3,227	7,646	—	—	—
1944	4,696	—	—	—	—	—

* Over 95 per cent. of the cases are matrimonial suits at the present time. 96 per cent. or 97 per cent. of the actions are successful.

2. Cases Handled by Services Divorce Department

A. *Services Section*

Year	Cases allocated to the Department	Petitions filed	Causes set down	Decrees Nisi obtained
1942 . .	1,749	795	380	152
1943 . .	3,424	2,125	986	848

B. *Civil Section*

Year	Cases allocated to the Department	Petitions filed	Causes set down	Decrees Nisi obtained
1943–4 . .	990	440	173	50

For Product Safety Concerns and Information please contact our EU
representative GPSR@taylorandfrancis.com
Taylor & Francis Verlag GmbH, Kaufingerstraße 24, 80331 München, Germany

www.ingramcontent.com/pod-product-compliance
Lightning Source LLC
LaVergne TN
LVHW021107300926
849160LV00009B/649
* 9 7 8 0 4 1 5 8 6 3 9 1 9 *